D1588263

CRAP TEAMS

CRAP TEAMS

GEOFF TIBBALLS

Michael O'Mara Books Limited

First published in Great Britain in 2005 by
Michael O'Mara Books Limited
9 Lion Yard
Tremadoc Road
London SW4 7NQ

This revised and updated edition first published in 2011

A CIP catalogue record for this book is available from the British Library.

Papers used by Michael O'Mara Books Limited are natural, recyclable products
made from wood grown in sustainable forests. The manufacturing processes
conform to the environmental regulations of the country of origin.

ISBN: 978-1-84317-598-8

1 3 5 7 9 10 8 6 4 2

Designed and typeset by www.envydesign.co.uk

Printed and bound in Singapore by Tien Wah Press Pte Ltd

www.mombooks.com

CONTENTS

Ipswich Town: 1994-95	50
Southampton: 1995-96	54
Bolton Wanderers: 1995-96	57
Fulham: 1995-96	60
Everton: 1997-98	63
Manchester City: 1997-98	66
Blackburn Rovers: 1998-99	68
Nottingham Forest: 1998-99	71
Glasgow Celtic: 1999-2000	74
Germany: 2000 European Championships Finals	77
Middlesbrough: 2000-01	80
Leicester City: 2001-02	83
France: 2002 World Cup Finals	86
Aston Villa: 2002-03	89
Liverpool: 2002-03	92
Scotland: 2002-04	95
Everton: 2003-04	98
Leeds United: 2003-04	101
Northern Ireland: 2004 European Championships Qualifiers	104

There is a lot to be said for supporting one of football's smaller clubs. It's rather like riding a 100 to 1 shot in the Derby or being a Dutch skier – expectation is lower than a chavette's IQ. As a result, defeat is invariably easier to take. Weekends aren't ruined, relationships aren't wrecked and the cat doesn't cower behind the sofa just because your team's new striker hits the target about as often as an archer with an uncontrollable twitch. But if you follow one of the Premier League big boys, it's a different story. At Chelsea, a run of two successive draws constitutes a crisis; at Rotherham, a crisis is when they run out of meat pies. So in a sport where money talks louder than Sir Alex Ferguson's famous hairdryer treatment and where even agents have agents, it is always refreshing to see the Premier League fat cats fail to get the cream.

As a humble Millwall supporter of fifty years' standing (and more recently sitting), it has therefore been a joy to recall those seasons when the top teams struggled miserably – when the trophy polisher at Old Trafford was made redundant due to lack of work, when the Gunners fired blanks, when Anfield attendances were so poor that Liverpool supporters did walk alone, and when there was more excitement at the Chelsea Flower Show than at Stamford Bridge.

Meanwhile on the international front, there is Scotland's greatest humiliation since their last great humiliation, England under 'Turnip' Taylor, the 'Wally with the Brolly' and the not-so-Fab Capello, the French farce that was the 2010 World Cup, and the summer when the only thing the Germans won was the race for the sunbeds.

So I would like to thank Kate Moore and the team at Michael O'Mara Books, as well as all of those overpaid footballers and underachieving managers, for making this book possible.

Geoff Tibballs, 2011

CHELSEA

1982-83

- ⊕ **League: 18th (Division 2)**
- ⊕ **FA Cup: 1-2 Derby County, round 4**
- ⊕ **League Cup: 0-2 Notts County, round 3**

By the season of 1978-79 the swinging Chelsea of Charlie Cooke, Alan Hudson, Ian Hutchinson and Peter Osgood were, rather like threepenny bits, jamboree bags and Hughie Green's career, consigned to the past. These stars had been replaced by functional, cut-price players; instead of King's Road boutiques, Chelsea were now browsing in their local pound shop. Relegation followed with ninety-two goals conceded, but then after three failed

THE LOWEST POINT IN CHELSEA'S HISTORY

attempts at returning to the top flight, manager John Neal vowed to get Chelsea out of the old Second Division. He very nearly did… by taking them down to the Third.

With relegation a distinct possibility until the first week in May, this season marked the lowest point in Chelsea's history – lower even than the release of 'Blue Is The Colour'. Under new owner Ken Bates these were dark days. The big summer signing was thirty-seven-year-old Bryan 'Pop' Robson, a fine player in his time but by 1982 his talent had receded as far as his hairline. Colin Lee, in his pre-bouffant days, led the attack alongside that fiery little scamp David Speedie. Some managers treated Speedie with kid gloves but others used rubber ones because he was such an irritant. In midfield Mike Fillery's silky skills were often hard to detect on cold evenings in Barnsley, Grimsby or Rotherham, while the fans never really took to winger Peter Rhoades-Brown, possibly because his name was so difficult to chant. 'Give us a hyphen' doesn't really have that ring to it. The one reassuring figure was long-serving, giant central defender Micky Droy, who was probably still around only because nobody could move him off the pitch.

With floating fans deciding that a sixth series of *Terry and June* offered more appeal than a trip to the Bridge, attendances dropped alarmingly. Only 7,808 turned up to see the biggest win of the season – a 6-0 hammering of Cambridge United. Neal kept promising a stirring finish but one win in the final eleven games left Chelsea needing a

⚽ ODDBALL

BEFORE MAKING HIS SENIOR DEBUT, CHELSEA DEFENDER CELESTINE BABAYARO WAS RULED OUT FOR SIX WEEKS AT THE START OF THE 1997–98 SEASON WITH A STRESS ANKLE FRACTURE ... SUSTAINED DURING ACROBATIC CELEBRATIONS TO MARK A GOAL IN A RESERVE TEAM FRIENDLY AT STEVENAGE.

fortuitous goal from Clive Walker at Bolton to provide the victory that guaranteed safety. Yet within a year Chelsea would be striding back to the top flight. If you had suggested that to fans in May 1983 they would have said it was about as likely as the club one day being taken over by a Russian multi-billionaire with a strange dummy-like grin.

Defender Micky Droy appeals to his teammates to show some semblance of talent.

BIRMINGHAM CITY

1985-86

- ⚽ **League: 21st (Division 1)**
- ⚽ **FA Cup: 1-2 Altrincham, round 3**
- ⚽ **League Cup: 0-3 Southampton, round 3 replay**

Back in the early eighties when law and order were taken seriously, persistent offenders were sent to one of three institutions – Parkhurst, Wormwood Scrubs or St Andrew's. Of these the last named, home of Birmingham City FC, was by far the toughest. Only the real hard cases were sent there – guys like Mick Harford, Julian Dicks, Martin Kuhl and Robert Hopkins. It was said they would nail a teammate's head to the dressing-room door just for underhitting a back pass or taking a last Rolo. Such was the reputation of these men for carrying out GBH on the pitch that players from other clubs used to dread getting a close-season call from the governor, Ron Saunders, making them an offer they couldn't refuse. The Krays deliberately pretended to be crap at football just so they wouldn't be sent to St Andrew's. By the summer of 1985 Harford had been released on parole, leaving Dicks and Kuhl to control the main block while Hopkins, in the number 11 shirt, was out on A Wing.

KNOCKED OUT OF THE CUP BY NON-LEAGUE ALTRINCHAM

A man who smiled only at coronations, Saunders had even fewer reasons to be cheerful that season. The Birmingham enforcers were struggling to leave their mark on the opposition and when, with a young David Seaman in goal, they were knocked out of the Cup by non-League Altrincham, Saunders was fired. His replacement, John Bond, was always remembered by fans long after he had left their club. Indeed in 1992 Burnley supporters were so keen to chat to him about old times that Bond had to watch his new club Shrewsbury's visit to Turf Moor disguised as a steward for fear of reprisals. Bond's first game in charge at St Andrew's brought a 1-0 win over Oxford – City's first victory since September – but it proved a false dawn. Bond said they'd turned the corner; the fans would have been happy just to win a corner. In the end only one team finished below Birmingham – neighbours

⚽ ODDBALL

BIRMINGHAM CITY DIDN'T COMPETE IN THE 1921-22 FA CUP ... BECAUSE THE CLUB FORGOT TO POST THE ENTRY FORM.

West Brom whose new manager was ... Ron Saunders. He thus had the distinction of presiding over the relegation of two teams in one season. For one year, at least, crime didn't pay.

Birmingham City player Robert Hopkins.
Would you mess with this man?

GLASGOW RANGERS

1985-86

- ☻ **League: 5th (Scottish Premier Division)**
- ☻ **Scottish FA Cup: 2-3 Hearts, round 3**
- ☻ **Scottish League Cup: 0-1 Hibernian, semi-final**
- ☻ **UEFA Cup: 1-2 (aggregate) Atletico Osasuna, round 1**

Jock Wallace first made Rangers players sick in 1967 when, as goalkeeper for little Berwick Rangers, he starred in the greatest giant-killing in the history of the Scottish Cup, when the minnows beat the Glasgow team 1-0. When he became manager at Ibrox in the 1970s he made the Rangers players sick again by forcing them to run up and down dunes in pre-season training. An ex-Army man whose love of discipline might have made him an ideal client for Cynthia Payne, Wallace led Rangers to two trebles. Although by Glasgow standards that's not much to drink, the fans loved him. He returned to the club for a second spell in the eighties and, while he still made Vlad the Impaler look like Julian Clary, he found it hard to repeat his earlier success. By the 1985-86 season Rangers hadn't won the League since 1978 or the Cup since 1981. And in Scotland that's almost as big a crime as taking a collection box … and putting money in it. The only consolation was that

WALLACE MADE VLAD THE IMPALER LOOK LIKE JULIAN CLARY

for the past two seasons Alex Ferguson's Aberdeen had prevented Celtic getting *their* hands on the League title. But with Celtic now battling it out with Hearts at the top and Rangers, who relied solely on the goals of Ally McCoist, languishing in mid-table, the knives were out for Wallace. He could have sharpened them on his tongue but instead, in April 1986 – the day after Rangers lost to Spurs in a friendly at Ibrox – he took one between the shoulder blades. Big Jock was on his way, to be replaced by another man not exactly from the Perry Como school of management, Graeme Souness.

Rangers finished the season with thirty-five points from thirty-six games – their lowest-ever tally. To add insult to injury, Celtic pipped Hearts for the title. To Rangers fans it was like your boss running off with your wife and then coming back to tell you what a great shag she was. Only worse.

⚽ ODDBALL

AFTER MISSING A SITTER AGAINST ABERDEEN IN 1991, RANGERS' CONTROVERSIAL STRIKER MO JOHNSTON WAS SO ANGRY WITH HIMSELF THAT HE PICKED UP A PIECE OF MUD AND HURLED IT TO THE GROUND. IN DOING SO, HE INJURED HIS BACK AND WAS FORCED TO MISS THE NEXT MATCH.

Rangers' goalie Chris Woods makes a rare save, in a season which saw the Scottish giants accrue just thirty-five points from thirty-six games.

MANCHESTER UNITED

1986-87

- ⚽ **League: 11th (Division 1)**
- ⚽ **FA Cup: 0-1 Coventry City, round 4**
- ⚽ **League Cup: 1-4 Southampton, round 4 replay**

After sacking Ron Atkinson in November 1986 in the wake of League Cup humiliation by Southampton, the United board reckoned they needed a quieter, more thoughtful, self-effacing manager, someone who could keep out of the headlines. So naturally they chose Alex Ferguson.

Back in the days when a pizza in the face would have changed his complexion, Fergie arrived at Old Trafford claiming that the League could still be won. What he failed to add was 'by Everton'. In fact, United finished thirty points adrift of the champions and below such superpowers as Wimbledon, Luton and Watford. Fergie was not helped by a strike force that even Arthur Scargill would have rejected. Mark Hughes had been sold to Barcelona in pre-season and his replacement, Peter Davenport, was already drawing unfavourable comparisons with another costly import from Nottingham Forest, Garry Birtles, who had failed to score in his first twenty-five league games for United in 1980-81. Frank Stapleton was nearing his sell-by date and

FERGIE ARRIVED CLAIMING THAT THE LEAGUE COULD STILL BE WON

⚽ ODDBALL

UNITED KEEPER ALEX STEPNEY SPENT SO MUCH TIME SHOUTING AT HIS TEAMMATES DURING A 1975 GAME WITH BIRMINGHAM CITY THAT HE WAS TAKEN TO HOSPITAL WITH A DISLOCATED JAW.

Terry Gibson was, frankly, short. When defenders talked of having him in their pocket, it wasn't necessarily a metaphor. Meanwhile in midfield Bryan Robson's shoulder was always likely to drop off at any minute.

Fortunately Fergie had an excuse for the team's indifferent form – the club's new £80,000 undersoil heating system which, to use the correct technical terminology, didn't work. Appearing to have been installed by the Chuckle Brothers, it left parts of the Old Trafford pitch as hard as a politician's heart and, when United were dumped out of the FA Cup by Coventry after the ball bobbled away from keeper Chris Turner on the slippery surface, it was the heating system that bore the brunt of Fergie's fury. That summer it was ripped out and has never been invited back to Old Trafford, not even for eighties' nights or testimonials. But it did mean that Fergie would have to come up with a fresh excuse when things went wrong. Just as he was racking his brains, the kit man passed and said: 'What do you reckon to grey shirts, boss?'

Man United boss Alex Ferguson – cocky as ever, but his team finished below such superpowers as Wimbledon, Luton and Watford in the 1986-87 season.

SUNDERLAND

1986-87

- ☺ **League: 20th (Division 2)**
- ☺ **FA Cup: 1-2 Wimbledon, round 3**
- ☺ **League Cup: 5-5 (lost on away goals) York City, round 1**

By 1986 Sunderland FC was not just a sleeping giant, it was practically comatose. Apart from the memorable FA Cup triumph of 1973, the once proud club had underachieved since the days when *Gone with the Wind* was showing at the local Gaumont. But this season would be worse than even the most pessimistic of fans could have feared, and would see Sunderland fall into the Third Division for the first time in

THE THIRD DIVISION FOR THE FIRST TIME IN THEIR HISTORY

their history. Yet the early omens were good and at the end of October the club were lying fifth. But then performances began to drop off faster than the front row at a Roger Whittaker concert.

In January manager Lawrie McMenemy agreed to take a sizeable pay cut but, despite the presence of experienced players such as George Burley, Eric Gates and Dave Swindlehurst, results failed to improve. A change of leadership was inevitable. Sunderland legend Bob Stokoe tried to work his old magic in a caretaker capacity but it would have needed Paul Daniels (assisted by the lovely Debbie

McGee) to get the club out of this mess. By finishing in twentieth position Sunderland entered the lottery of the newly introduced play-offs, where they went out on away goals to Gillingham and were relegated. Things were shabbier than Stokoe's famous raincoat. Meanwhile the board were at their wits' end. For some members it had not been a long journey.

⚽ ODDBALL

SUNDERLAND FAN STEPHEN JONES DESERTED HIS VERY NEW WIFE TO WATCH HIS TEAM PLAY GRIMSBY IN 1998-99. HE LEFT THE WEDDING RECEPTION AT WINGATE, COUNTY DURHAM, AND ORDERED THE LIMOUSINE CHAUFFEUR TO DRIVE HIM, HIS BEST MAN AND THE USHERS TO THE STADIUM OF LIGHT. ANOTHER TWENTY-EIGHT GUESTS FOLLOWED IN A MINI-BUS. BUOYED BY A 3-1 WIN, HE RETURNED TO THE RECEPTION – AND HIS UNDERSTANDING BRIDE – AFTER THE GAME.

Caretaker manager Bob Stokoe has every right to look shifty as he oversees the demise of Sunderland in their worst-ever season.

TOTTENHAM HOTSPUR

1987-88

- ⚽ **League: 13th (Division 1)**
- ⚽ **FA Cup: 1-2 Port Vale, round 4**
- ⚽ **League Cup: 1-2 Aston Villa, round 3**

Rather like Dennis Bergkamp certain London teams have not always travelled well. On a boggy pitch any northern side used to fancy their chances against West Ham or their equally cultured capital cousins. So, when Spurs were drawn to visit Port Vale in the FA Cup at the end of January 1988, alarm bells started ringing. Vale may have been languishing in eighteenth place in Division Three but the pitch was sure to be stickier than a teenage boy's

AN INAUSPICIOUS START FOR NEW MANAGER TERRY VENABLES

copy of *Knave*. And the word on the streets was that Spurs did not like it up 'em. This was an occasion that called for a bear of a man and in their line-up Spurs had a player who fitted that description. Chris Waddle was indeed a bear, but only in the sense that he hibernated in winter. When the going got muddy, you would rather have had Edmund Blackadder with you in the trenches than Waddle. At the other extreme Spurs could call upon Neil Ruddock who, even at that tender age, was bulky enough to warrant diversion signs whenever he fell over.

Spurs' predictable defeat capped an

inauspicious start for new manager Terry Venables, fresh from topping up his tan in Barcelona. Beaten Cup finalists the previous season, Spurs had lost Glenn Hoddle to Monaco in the summer and manager David Pleat to the tabloids in October, following lurid allegations about his one-man crusade to make Luton worth visiting.

Venables's response to the subsequent slump was to sign goalkeeper Bobby Mimms, striker Paul Walsh and, naturally, Terry Fenwick, a recurring theme of his management career In the same way that an alcoholic orders another drink, Venables would send for Terry Fenwick. He also jettisoned two of Pleat's last signings, the ex-Forest pair of Chris Fairclough and Dutchman Johnny Metgod (pronounced 'Met-hod', which must have been confusing for Amsterdam churchgoers). Alas, Spurs fans could no longer worship their own Hod

⚽ ODDBALL

SPURS FORWARDS LES FERDINAND AND RUEL FOX MISSED THE START OF THE SECOND HALF AT NEWCASTLE IN 1997 AFTER GETTING THEMSELVES LOCKED IN THE TOILET.

and, without Glenn's artistry, the team struggled. Luckily El Tel promised a brighter future. But didn't he always?

Goalkeeper Bobby Mimms, pointing the way to where Spurs' hopes went.

PORTSMOUTH

1987-88

- ☺ **League: 19th (Division 1)**
- ☺ **FA Cup: 1-3 Luton Town, round 6**
- ☺ **League Cup: 2-6 (aggregate) Swindon Town, round 2**

The history of football is littered with truly great players who have struggled as managers – Billy Wright, Bobby Moore, Bobby Charlton, er … Trevor Francis. To that list has to be added Alan Ball, a genuine enthusiast whose tendency to wear his heart on his sleeve amazed fans and doctors alike. Bally did enjoy the occasional triumph – such as guiding Portsmouth to the Second Division title in 1987 – but as sure as night follows day, his success would be followed almost immediately by disaster. Maybe part of the reason lay with the fact that, because of his high-pitched voice, only dogs could hear his pre-match instructions.

After leading Pompey back to the top flight for the first time in twenty-eight years, Ball's feet hardly touched the ground. A set of lower chairs helped but it soon became apparent that the team was ill equipped for the task in hand. They would have been out of their depth in the shallow end of the local swimming pool. The attack was led by thirty-four-year-old Paul Mariner and Micky 'Sumo' Quinn – who was to

SUCCESS WOULD BE FOLLOWED IMMEDIATELY BY DISASTER

⚽ ODDBALL

IN 1994 PORTSMOUTH FAN MIKE HALL SAID HE WAS GOING TO SUE THE LEAGUE FOR HIS TICKET MONEY AND TRAVEL COSTS FOR WHAT HE CLAIMED WAS A WASTED TRIP TO OLDHAM TO SEE POMPEY BEATEN BY TWO DISPUTED PENALTIES.

dieting what Brian Sewell is to army camouflage trousers. In fact the sight of Quinn is believed to have inspired the terrace craze for inflatables. To bolster his strike force Ball recruited Ian Baird from Leeds for £385,000 but, when the opening game at Fratton Park ended in a 3-0 defeat to Chelsea, and two matches later Pompey were mauled 6-0 at Highbury, it indicated a long winter ahead.

Off the field the club's assets were temporarily frozen by the bank, forcing chairman John Deacon to pay the players out of his own pocket. He must have been tempted to put the money to better use – such as on the 2.30 at Catterick. A closing run of one win in thirteen condemned Portsmouth to a quick return to Division Two, but Ball was always assured of a warm welcome in the city. Then again, so was Joan of Arc at Rouen.

Even Ian Baird's impressive acrobatic displays weren't enough to save Portsmouth from relegation.

NEWCASTLE UNITED

1988-89

- ☺ **League: 20th (Division 1)**
- ☺ **FA Cup: 0-1 Watford, round 3**
- ☺ **League Cup: 2-4 (aggregate) Southampton, round 2**

Before foreign players became such a fashion accessory that every top British club had to have at least a dozen of them it was only a select few that ventured to these shores. With fond memories of Argentinians Ossie Ardiles and Ricky Villa at Spurs, Newcastle splashed out £575,000 on Brazilian centre-forward Mirandinha, reasoning that the new undersoil heating at St James' Park would help him acclimatize. He was bought to pacify fans mourning the sale of Peter Beardsley and Chris Waddle who were scared that their beloved Gazza would soon follow suit. Their worst fears were realized in the summer of 1988 when Paul Gascoigne joined Spurs for £2m. Big mistake: everyone knows that black and white stripes take pounds off you. Early next season he returned to Tyneside with his new team and was subjected to constant jeers of 'Fattie'. At least there was nothing wrong with the Newcastle fans' eyesight.

Meanwhile Mirandinha was suffering from enough ailments to warrant a special

A SPLINTER WAS LIABLE TO KEEP MIRANDINHA OUT FOR SIX WEEKS

⚽ ODDBALL

WHEN GAZZA'S NEW TEAM SPURS VISITED NEWCASTLE ON THE SECOND SATURDAY OF THE 1988-89 SEASON, THE NEWCASTLE OLD BOY WAS BOMBARDED WITH MARS BARS.

edition of *The Lancet*. A splinter was liable to keep him out for six weeks while a nagging cold was deemed career threatening. When he did make it on to the pitch he appeared determined to do everything himself, thus proving to be the only Latin American male incapable of making a pass. In October the team's desperate form cost manager Willie McFaul his job. His successor, the experienced Jim Smith, soon consigned the costly Brazilian to the 'waste of money' bin where he joined Smith's bottle of anti-dandruff shampoo. When United were duly relegated after finishing bottom, Mirandinha knew his days were numbered. He had said he wanted to use the money he made in Newcastle to buy a pig farm outside Sao Paulo. A few of its inmates would need to fly before he was ever declared a local hero back on Tyneside.

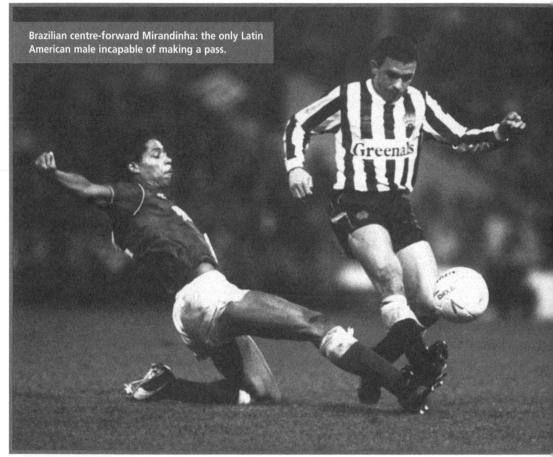

Brazilian centre-forward Mirandinha: the only Latin American male incapable of making a pass.

CHARLTON ATHLETIC

1989-90

- ☺ **League: 19th (Division 1)**
- ☺ **FA Cup: 0-1 West Bromwich Albion, round 4**
- ☺ **League Cup: 0-1 Southampton, round 3**

Between 1985 and 1992 a strange group of people wearing red and white anoraks could be seen roaming the streets of south and east London in search of a home. Without so much as a bundle of *Big Issues* to their name, they were small in number, often downcast but unfailingly polite. They were Charlton supporters. These shy nomads who, like the team they followed, tended to panic when a camera was pointed at them, came into being after

CHARLTON WERE THE CUCKOOS OF FOOTBALL

Charlton went into administration and were forced to move from The Valley. For the next seven years Charlton wandered the wilderness, sharing first with Crystal Palace at Selhurst Park and then with West Ham at Upton Park. They were the cuckoos of football. Clubs became wise to their tactics.

Staff at other London grounds always ensured their gates were locked at night in case Charlton had moved in by the morning.

Season 1989-90 saw Charlton lodging at Selhurst Park. Although manager Lennie Lawrence had done a sterling job in such difficult circumstances, it was widely accepted that Charlton were no more likely to be seen challenging for honours than Jeremy Clarkson would appear in a floral pinafore and a pair of Marigolds. In a bid to preserve their tenuously held top-flight status, they signed defender Joe McLaughlin from Chelsea for £600,000 in pre-season but the real problems lay at the other end of the pitch where striker Paul Williams was woefully lacking in support. Which brings us to Carl Leaburn, the sort of cult hero who comes along maybe once in a lifetime. At 6ft 3in Leaburn should have been better in the air than easyJet but far from proving a real handful for defenders, his goals were as rare as an Alaskan heatwave. He had previously managed just three in fifty-two games and maintained the run by failing to score in his eight starts in 1989-90. But the crowd loved him … in the same way that owners love a three-legged greyhound. Leaburn's boundless enthusiasm

⚽ ODDBALL

WHEN CHARLTON BEAT WEST BROM IN FRONT OF THE CAMERAS ON 5 FEBRUARY 1995, IT WAS THEIR FIRST VICTORY ON LIVE TELEVISION SINCE THE 1947 FA CUP FINAL.

was matched only by his ineptitude. What with Robert Lee contributing one goal from thirty-seven appearances, Charlton struggled all season. As defeat followed defeat, heads began to drop faster than they did at the height of the French Revolution. With just thirty-one goals from thirty-eight games, Charlton finished second from bottom – and thirteen points from safety – despite notable victories over Chelsea and Manchester United.

However it was not all doom and gloom for Charlton that season. For a start, neighbours Millwall were the only team worse than them in the First Division. Also, stung by Greenwich Council's refusal to allow planning permission for the Valley, Charlton supporters decided to fight the council at the local elections in May 1990. There were rumours that Carl Leaburn was standing … since standing was very much his forte on the pitch. Even without him the Valley Party picked up 14,838 votes and managed to unseat the chairman of the planning committee! Two months later planning permission was finally granted for the derelict Valley and although Charlton didn't actually move back until the end of 1992, at least it gave them time to think about the colour scheme and whether to have the executive boxes facing the pitch.

Charlton striker Carl Leaburn was a cult hero for his enthusiastic failure to score, his goals were as rare as an Alaskan heatwave.

WEST HAM UNITED

1991-92

- ✪ **League: 22nd (Division 1)**
- ✪ **FA Cup: 2-3 Sunderland, round 5 replay**
- ✪ **League Cup: 1-2 Norwich City, round 4**

What West Ham really needed, as they struggled in the bottom three for most of the season, was Billy Bonds the player. Unfortunately they got Billy Bonds the manager. In midfield Bonds had been a fearless swash-buckling pirate, but in the managerial dugout that season he proved about as bold and effective as Captain Pugwash.

As it happened, it was in midfield that the Hammers' major problems lay. The chief creative attacking forces, Stuart Slater and Ian Bishop, played forty-one games apiece

DOT COTTON WAS THINKING OF APPLYING FOR THE JOB OF HAMMERS' MANAGER

and contributed one goal between them. Joe Bugner would have packed more goalmouth punch. With Second Division Charlton sharing Upton Park for the season, a visiting Martian would have been hard pushed to tell which team was West Ham, which was Charlton and which was the Dagenham Girl Pipers. The Hammers' poor League form transferred itself to the FA Cup, where they needed two attempts to scrape past Conference team Farnborough despite both games being staged at Upton Park. As West Ham's crisis mirrored that of Walford Town's in *EastEnders*, word had it that Dot Cotton was thinking of applying for the job of Hammers' manager, provided she could combine it with working at the launderette. Meanwhile West Ham continued to air their dirty washing in public and in February 200 fans staged a pitch protest against the club's bond scheme, although some turned up only because they had heard it was an anti-Bonds rally.

Whereas most clubs change their manager more often than Jim Royle changes his underpants, West Ham had always bucked that trend. Consequently Bonds remained in charge despite relegation and repaid the board's faith by taking the team straight back up. But in August 1994, with Bonds deciding he no longer needed the hassle, West Ham decided they no longer needed him. After twenty-seven years together it was the saddest parting since Bobby Charlton's combover.

⚽ ODDBALL

WEST HAM'S IAN WRIGHT WAS FINED AND BANNED FOR THREE MATCHES FOR TRASHING REFEREE ROB HARRIS'S ROOM AFTER BEING SENT OFF AGAINST LEEDS UNITED IN 1999.

Long-standing West Ham man Billy Bonds. If only his management style had matched his on-pitch prowess.

England
1992 EUROPEAN CHAMPIONSHIPS FINALS

Ah, 1992, the Chinese year of the Turnip. After Graham Taylor was depicted by *The Sun* as a root vegetable following England's depressing exit from the European Championships, hunting him became a national pastime. Thankfully this entertainment has now been restricted and can be done by only two journalists at a time, meaning editors must call off a pack of newshounds. Furthermore they can follow only the scent of Taylor, not the man himself.

Many feel that the manager got a raw deal over the England job. It wasn't his fault

GAMES SO BAD EVEN THE BALLBOYS WERE BOOED OFF

that England had produced hardly any world-class players since 1966. Already deprived of Paul Gascoigne, John Barnes, Bryan Robson and Mark Wright, Taylor didn't have to dig much deeper to start scraping bottoms of barrels, caps being awarded to the likes of Keith Curle, Carlton Palmer, Andy Sinton and Tony Daley. The pool of talent barely came up to your ankles. Even the absent Lee Dixon was missed. Des Walker was a shadow of his former self and Gary Lineker had announced that he was retiring after the finals. Instead of Sinton and Daley

⚽ ODDBALL

UNOFFICIAL ENGLAND TEAM FAITH-HEALER EILEEN DREWERY CLAIMED THAT SHE PREVENTED IAN WRIGHT SCORING IN A 1997 WORLD CUP QUALIFIER IN ITALY (HE HIT THE POST IN THE LAST MINUTE) FOR FEAR THAT A GOAL MIGHT HAVE SPARKED CROWD TROUBLE.

he would be more concerned with cheese and onion.

If the qualifying performances were lacklustre (seven goals from six games), England reserved their worst for the finals in Sweden. England were as drab and colourless as a November afternoon in Doncaster. Following goalless draws against Denmark and France (games so bad even the ballboys were booed off), England faced Sweden. David Platt raised false hopes early on but the hosts fought back

and, after Taylor had controversially replaced Lineker in his last international with Arsenal's Alan Smith, Tomas Brolin sank England. Brolin would later put on enough weight to sink a small battleship. Taylor was roundly pilloried, not least for the perceived snub to Lineker that denied him the chance of equalling Bobby Charlton's England goalscoring record. It was like kicking away the Queen Mother's walking stick. Taylor's reputation never recovered but Dame Fortune had rarely smiled upon him. Fast forward ten years and England's prospects under new management at the World Cup would founder because sadly 2002 was not the Chinese year of the Love Rat.

Housewives' favourite Gary Lineker: Euro '92 was his international swansong but England were more like ugly ducklings throughout the championships.

BIRMINGHAM CITY

1993-94

- ⚽ **League: 22nd (Division 1)**
- ⚽ **FA Cup: 1-2 Kidderminster Harriers, round 3**
- ⚽ **League Cup: 0-2 (aggregate) Aston Villa, round 2**

Barry Fry is one of those guys whom football supporters love … as long as he's not managing their club. A total enthusiast – and with the heart attacks to prove it – Fry breezes in and out of clubs like a chubby tornado, making headlines and leaving chaos and confusion in his wake. His friends say he's infectious … but so was the Black Death. Blessed with the poise and elegance of a dodgy second-hand car dealer, Fry has always enjoyed nothing more than

BARRY FRY IS INFECTIOUS … BUT SO WAS THE BLACK DEATH

dabbling in the transfer market. Constantly on the lookout for a bargain, he would sign a player, give him a few games – but then see an even better bargain on offer and sign him too. Consequently Birmingham, in common with Fry's other clubs, operated a revolving door policy where players would be shipped in and out frequently, barely staying long enough to acquire their own peg in the dressing room.

Fry arrived at St Andrew's in place of Terry Cooper in December 1993. The team were already struggling in soccer's second tier but the bullish Bazza reckoned he could turn things around if he was allowed to bring in a few players. By the end of the season

⚽ ODDBALL

WHEN HE WAS MANAGER OF BARNET, BARRY FRY WAS ONCE SEEN MOWING THE UNDERHILL PITCH BY MOONLIGHT AT FOUR O'CLOCK IN THE MORNING. HE TOLD INVESTIGATING POLICE OFFICERS THAT HE WAS SO WORKED UP ABOUT THAT AFTERNOON'S MATCH THAT HE COULDN'T SLEEP AND HAD DECIDED TO DO SOMETHING USEFUL INSTEAD.

Birmingham had used a staggering forty players in their unsuccessful fight against the drop with only one – striker Andy Saville – making more than thirty appearances. By contrast champions Crystal Palace used only twenty-two in the course of the season. Birmingham players often met their teammates for the first time on match days – sometimes, one suspected, while the coin was being tossed. It was more like speed dating than football management.

In Fry's first month at the club alone he spent £1.27 million on nine new players, but failed to find a drawing, let alone a winning, formula. Then Birmingham were paired with neighbours Kidderminster Harriers of the Conference in the third round of the FA Cup. Although Kidderminster had never beaten a League club in their 108-year history, Fry feared the worst and, sure enough, the visitors – aided by a Saville penalty miss – pulled off the shock of the round. Fry was beside himself, although with his girth, it was sometimes an optical illusion. At the final reckoning Birmingham were relegated on goal difference beneath local rivals West Brom. And Fry was probably still telling the board that a couple more new signings would have made all the difference …

Birmingham City manager Barry Fry – a football legend, but for all the wrong reasons.

ARSENAL

1994-95

- ⚽ **League: 12th (Premiership)**
- ⚽ **FA Cup: 0-2 Millwall, round 3 replay**
- ⚽ **League Cup: 0-1 Liverpool, round 5**
- ⚽ **European Cup-Winners' Cup: 1-2 Real Zaragoza, final**

The Highbury faithful were taking bets on which would happen first: the colonization of Mars, Lord Lucan presenting *Wish You Were Here?* or a John Jensen goal for Arsenal. The Danish midfielder had gone ninety-seven scoreless games for the Gunners until, on the last day of 1994, he finally broke his duck during the 3-1 home defeat by Queens Park Rangers. News of Jensen's goal sent shock waves through the world. The immediate impact was that Arsenal lost to Spurs at White Hart Lane before being dumped out of the Cup by First Division Millwall, and Robbie Williams left Take That.

Jensen's joy was about the only bright spot in a miserable season for Arsenal. Paul Merson confessed to drink, drug and gambling problems. (What's the difference between Paul Merson and a can of Coca-Cola? – One's red and white and full of coke, the other's a soft drinks container.) And manager George Graham was sacked over financial irregularities after opening more envelopes than you see on Oscars night. His assistant, Stewart Houston, took over the

NOTHING BECKONED BEYOND MID-TABLE MEDIOCRITY

☺ ODDBALL

AFTER SCORING THE WINNER IN THE 1993 COCA-COLA CUP FINAL YOUNG ARSENAL MIDFIELDER STEVE MORROW BROKE HIS ARM WHEN, IN THE POST-MATCH CELEBRATIONS, SKIPPER TONY ADAMS PUT HIM OVER HIS SHOULDER AND ACCIDENTALLY DROPPED HIM.

reins and promptly steered Arsenal to a first home win in four months, but nothing beckoned beyond mid-table mediocrity. Even the rock of the team's previous success – the synchronized offside back four of Lee Dixon, Steve Bould, Tony Adams and Nigel Winterburn – was starting to show cracks. And when Andy Linighan was forced to step in, it was noticeable that he was always

Goalie David Seaman watches as yet another ball sails past him into the net. It was a sight much seen all season.

that split second behind the other three when raising his hand to appeal. He just hadn't mastered the routine. It was much the same when Jenny first replaced Kerry in Atomic Kitten.

Yet against all the odds there was hope of a trophy when Arsenal travelled to Paris for the European Cup-Winners' Cup final against Spain's Real Zaragoza. However, in the last minute of extra-time with the score at 1-1, Nayim – a former Spurs player to boot – lobbed David Seaman from 50 yards. The goalkeeper flapped and back-pedalled in vain. Somewhere in the stand a Mr Ronaldinho was taking notes …

IPSWICH TOWN

1994-95

- ☺ **League: 22nd (Premiership)**
- ☺ **FA Cup: 1-2 Wrexham, round 3**
- ☺ **League Cup: 0-4 Bolton (aggregate), round 2**

With most local derbies you can understand the animosity. Rangers versus Celtic represents bigoted, sectarian hatred; Southampton and Portsmouth stems from Navy rivalry; in Liverpool, Manchester, Sheffield, Bristol etc. it is about divisions and loyalties within the city. But Ipswich and Norwich, what's that all about? Neither place could be termed a soccer hotbed. 'Canaries'? It's not quite in the same league as 'Lions', 'Tigers' or even 'Seagulls'.

JEFFREY ARCHER HAD A BETTER DEFENCE THAN IPSWICH

What's the worst thing a canary can do to you? Sing out of tune? And, when your chief cheerleader is a middle-England TV cook, we're not exactly talking tribal warfare. So, to the outsider at least, this simmering feud seems nothing more than a spat between two old farmers as to who has the better marrow at the local vegetable show.

The 1994-95 season saw both teams relegated from the Premiership but Norwich City held local bragging rights, not only by finishing two places above Ipswich but also by completing the double over them. Norwich were not exactly unique in that respect, since Jeffrey Archer had a better defence than Ipswich. They conceded a staggering ninety-three goals – more than two a game – to make goalkeeper Craig Forrest the busiest man in East Anglia (apart from the owner of the local inbreeding farm). With things looking blacker than a Goth wedding, manager John Lyall received the traditional pre-Christmas sack from Santa and was replaced by George Burley. Defeat in the Cup to Second Division Wrexham was followed by a run of eight straight defeats, including a 9-0 mauling at Old Trafford. Ian Marshall, who always looked like the lost member of Spinal Tap, managed a couple of goals late in the season but Ipswich's fate had long been sealed. Hostilities would be renewed in Division One with basted turkeys at dawn.

⚽ ODDBALL

WHEN IPSWICH MANAGER JOE ROYLE BECAME BOSS OF OLDHAM ATHLETIC IN 1982, HE ARRIVED FOR HIS FIRST DAY AT WORK IN THE CAB OF A COAL LORRY. HE HAD BEEN FORCED TO HITCH A LIFT AFTER HIS CAR BROKE DOWN ON THE WAY TO BOUNDARY PARK.

Ipswich vs Norwich – as fierce as it gets in East Anglia, as Jon Newsome (left) and Ian Marshall battle it out for the ball.

SOUTHAMPTON

1995-96

- ⚽ League: 17th (Premiership)
- ⚽ FA Cup: 2-6 Tottenham Hotspur, round 5 replay
- ⚽ League Cup: 1-2 Reading, round 4

When Alan Ball left Southampton to become Manchester City's problem, Dave Merrington, coach at The Dell for eleven years, was elevated to manager. As for Stevie Wonder on a ladder, the step up is notoriously difficult and, while Ball may not have cast the longest of shadows, even he proved a tough act for Merrington to follow.

SAINTS HOVERED DANGEROUSLY ABOVE THE RELEGATION PLACES

As usual the team's hopes rested firmly on the shoulders of Matt Le Tissier, viewed by Saints fans as the best news to come out of the Channel Islands since Mike and Bernie Winters announced they were no longer doing summer seasons. Le Tissier was supremely gifted. When God dealt out the talent among footballers, you didn't have to look far to see who got Carlton Palmer's share. Only a leper could drop a shoulder like Le Tissier. But the great man managed only seven League goals in 1995-96 (three of them penalties), as a result of which Saints hovered dangerously above the relegation places. Ultimately it needed a goalless draw at home to Wimbledon in the final game of the season to secure Southampton's safety on goal difference ahead of … Manchester City. It was good to

Not even the talents of Matt Le Tissier could help Southampton this season … particularly when he insisted on playing 'piggy in the middle' with the Magpies.

☻ ODDBALL

AFTER BREAKING HIS ARM IN A MATCH AT LEICESTER IN 1998-99 SOUTHAMPTON DEFENDER FRANCIS BENALI REPEATED THE FEAT A MONTH LATER WHILE SWEEPING UP LEAVES IN HIS GARDEN.

know that Ball hadn't lost his touch. Yet the most eventful game of the season was a 6-2 home defeat by Spurs in the Cup, courtesy of a Ronny Rosenthal hat-trick – a remarkable feat in itself as Devon Loch was a better finisher than Rosenthal.

Although Merrington had kept the team up, he was not invited to stay on as manager. But in one respect, he fared better than his many successors at Southampton. After all, what could be worse than being sacked by a bloke called Rupert?

BOLTON WANDERERS

1995-96

- ☺ League: 20th (Premiership)
- ☺ FA Cup: 0-1 Leeds United, round 4
- ☺ League Cup: 2-3 (on penalties) Norwich City, round 4 replay

As with all businesses, football goes through certain vogues. There have been crazes for plastic pitches, snoods, the diamond formation, signing American internationals just because they've got over a hundred caps. Even Fabio Capello was once all the rage. Similarly there was a time when joint managers were in fashion. It all started with Alan Curbishley and Steve Gritt at Charlton and, when that proved a short-term success, others followed suit, usually with calamitous consequences. For just as two heads are better than one, too many cooks spoil the broth. A case in point was the partnership of former Derby and England teammates Roy McFarland and Colin Todd at Bolton Wanderers in 1995. What they lacked in managerial experience at the highest level they made up for with immaculate grooming. Todd, in particular, could have modelled blazers in a Littlewoods catalogue. He would no more be seen sporting a mullet than Sam Allardyce would be seen with a ponytail or Tony Adams would be seen with a manager-of-the-month award.

BOLTON WERE LIKE WORZEL GUMMIDGE – A SHAMBOLIC OUTFIT

⚽ ODDBALL

IN MAY 2003 REVEREND ROGER OLDFIELD, A BOLTON SUPPORTER FOR THIRTY YEARS, HELD A SPECIAL SERVICE, OFFERING PRAYERS FOR THE CLUB TO AVOID RELEGATION. ALL ATTENDEES WERE GIVEN ORANGES HALFWAY THROUGH THE SERVICE WHILE A SAM ALLARDYCE LOOKALIKE FROM THE CONGREGATION BARKED ORDERS FROM A MAKESHIFT DUGOUT AT THE FRONT OF THE CHURCH.

Alas, Bolton, on their return to the top flight, were more like Worzel Gummidge – a shambolic outfit whose victory over Wimbledon on 13 January was only their third win of the season. Although the management team had paid a club record £1.5m for Barnsley defender Gerry Taggart, it was a lack of goals that sounded Bolton's death knell. The strike force of John McGinlay, Fabian De Freitas and Nathan Blake carried all the menace of a Tim Henman snarl. With Wanderers eight points adrift at the bottom, McFarland was relieved of his duties in January, allowing Todd to take sole charge. Around that time Tony Blair was promising 'Things can only get better'. He had obviously not been to Bolton. For Wanderers finished bottom of the Premiership, having lost twenty-five of their thirty-eight games. Even so, theirs wasn't the worst record that year. Gina G saw to that.

Bolton clash with Leeds in the FA Cup fourth round.

FULHAM

1995-96

- League: 18th (Division 3)
- FA Cup: 1-2 Shrewsbury, round 3 replay
- League Cup: 1-7 (aggregate) Wolverhampton Wanderers, round 2

Before the Harrods van parked outside the main entrance of Craven Cottage, Fulham were everyone's favourite aunt: delightfully dotty, always a welcome visitor and never likely to give you a beating. But years of neglect and the onset of Alzheimer's – she couldn't remember when she'd last won a trophy – had left the old girl at serious risk of being sectioned in the Conference. The man charged with keeping away the men in white coats was Ian Branfoot, who had previously been hounded out of Southampton. Indeed he could not have been more reviled by fans at The Dell had he been waving a Portsmouth season ticket.

Bringing all the tact of Trinny and Susannah to Craven Cottage, Branfoot set about matters in a typically no-nonsense fashion. He overhauled the playing staff, bringing in so many ageing players that Saga thought about becoming the shirt sponsor. It did not go unnoticed that a number of the recruits had a spell with Southampton on their CV. He favoured direct football, destined, it seemed, to take Fulham directly to the bottom of the table.

SAGA THOUGHT ABOUT BECOMING THE SHIRT SPONSOR

Manager Ian Branfoot confidently displays an armpit free from sweat patch. He may have kept his cool; his job was another matter.

Without a win for twelve games, Branfoot was rapidly becoming as unpopular as he had been at Southampton – except that Fulham fans were generally too polite to resort to abusive threats. When it came to radical revolution they favoured the Sergeant Wilson approach.

With the team's fortunes at their lowest ebb, they somehow conjured up a 7-0 hammering of Second Division Swansea in the first round of the FA Cup. The result came as such a shock that the obituaries column in the following week's *Fulham & Hammersmith Chronicle* was double its normal length. The expected improvement in form didn't follow, however, and in February 1996 Branfoot stepped aside to allow player-coach Micky Adams to become the League's youngest boss.

Adams steadied the ship to preserve League status and went on to lead Fulham

⚽ ODDBALL

SENEGAL MIDFIELDER PAPA BOUBA DIOP REPORTEDLY PERFORMED A VOODOO CEREMONY INVOLVING THE SPRINKLING OF ANIMAL BLOOD AROUND THE CRAVEN COTTAGE PITCH IN AN ATTEMPT TO PUT THE MAGIC BACK INTO FULHAM'S 2004-05 SEASON.

to promotion in 1997. But when his Harrods hamper arrived, it contained his P45. And not even a Scotch egg.

EVERTON

1997-98

- ☺ **League: 17th (Premiership)**
- ☺ **FA Cup: 0-1 Newcastle, round 3**
- ☺ **League Cup: 1-4 Coventry, round 3**

There are four great mysteries in life. Why did God give men nipples? How does the guy who drives the snowplough get to work? Why do people eat cooked breakfasts off the open pages of library books? And how have Everton managed to stay in the top division for over fifty years?

For too many seasons, particularly in the 1990s, the Toffeemen cheated the drop at the last minute, invariably owing their survival to one man – Welsh goalkeeper Neville Southall. But by 1997 the former dustman, whose general demeanour suggested he still rummaged in bins on his days off, was nearing the end of his Everton career. Manager Howard Kendall was back for an unprecedented third term, something that the American constitution wisely ensured was later denied to George W. Bush. Kendall relied on the little and large strike force of Nick Barmby and Duncan Ferguson but there were times when Syd and Eddie themselves would not have looked out of place in the Everton attack. Ferguson, for all his physical threat, has never been a prolific goalscorer while Barmby must be the only person in Britain to be homesick for Hull.

EVERTON WERE JUST LIKE THE TITANIC

...ton stalwart Duncan Ferguson dramatically uproots
...castle's Alessandro Pistone.

This was to prove an especially traumatic season for Evertonians, a Gary Speed penalty against Leicester just before Christmas ending a run of eight games without a win. At least there would be something to celebrate that Christmas – and to compensate for the Sonia CD in their stocking.

While fans vented their anger at chairman Peter Johnson rather than Kendall, the team succeeded where Robert Maxwell had failed by just about keeping their heads above water. It all boiled down to the final game – at home to Coventry. Although Barmby missed a penalty, a 1-1 draw was enough to keep Everton up on goal difference, thanks to Chelsea's victory over Bolton. Before the kick-off against Coventry, Everton women's team took a bow for winning their league and the club's youth team were applauded for winning the FA Youth Cup. As one wag remarked, Everton were just like the *Titanic* – women and children first. He did not need to add … and sinking fast.

☻ ODDBALL

DESPERATE FOR A TRANSFER, EVERTON KEEPER NEVILLE SOUTHALL STAGED A HALF-TIME PROTEST DURING A 1990 MATCH WITH LEEDS. WHILE HIS TEAMMATES WERE IN THE DRESSING ROOM, A MOROSE SOUTHALL SAT ALONE ON THE PITCH AT THE FOOT OF A GOALPOST.

MANCHESTER CITY

1997-98

- ⚽ **League: 22nd (Division 1)**
- ⚽ **FA Cup: 1-2 West Ham, round 4**
- ⚽ **League Cup: 2-4 (on penalties) Blackpool, round 1**

You only have to look at some celebrities to tell which team they support. Actor Alan Davies appears calm and laid-back because he supports Arsenal; Jo Brand needs a great sense of humour because she follows Crystal Palace; Angus Deayton has an air of superiority because he supports Manchester United; and the Gallagher brothers are psychotic because they support Manchester City. Ever since the days of Joe Mercer and Malcolm Allison, following City

ONLY CITY COULD SCORE FIVE AND GO DOWN

has been more of a ghost train than a rollercoaster simply because you never know what's lurking round the corner. At their best, to paraphrase Swiss Toni, watching City was like making love to a beautiful woman – exciting, breathtaking and dangerous; at their worst it was like making love to an old slapper – painful, unhealthy and best done with your eyes shut. The best bit was the break when you changed ends.

The 1997-98 season saw City playing in the second tier. Their manager was Frank Clark, a man with the permanent expression of a benevolent bloodhound. His dour voice gave the impression that he was better suited to making station announcements at Manchester Piccadilly than delivering rousing Churchillian speeches at half-time. With City facing relegation to the third grade for the first time in their 111-year history, Clark was replaced in February by the admirable Joe Royle. Some people say Royle has a chip on his shoulder, others say that's because he's got a potato for a head. But, despite signing assorted Russians and Georgians whose main functions were to keep their one star player, Georgi Kinkladze, company and to use up the tricky consonants in Soccer Scrabble, City were relegated. Typically inconsistent, they won their final game 5-2 at Stoke, sending both teams down. Their fans were left to reflect that only Manchester City could score five and go down.

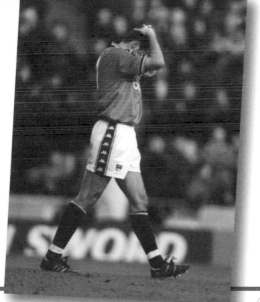

Uwe Rösler: not initiating an upbeat team display of 'Heads, Shoulders, Knees and Toes', but showing his dejection after missing a penalty.

⚽ ODDBALL

IN MARCH 1999 A DISENCHANTED MANCHESTER CITY FAN THREW AN ASTHMA INHALER ON TO THE MAINE ROAD PITCH DURING A FEEBLE DRAW WITH NORTHAMPTON TOWN.

BLACKBURN ROVERS

1998-99

- ⚽ **League: 19th (Premiership)**
- ⚽ **FA Cup: 0-1 Newcastle United, round 5 replay**
- ⚽ **League Cup: 0-1 Leicester City, round 5**
- ⚽ **UEFA Cup: 2-3 (aggregate) Lyon, round 1**

Doctor Who, Lee Mack and Jack Straw. Apart from being three people who have never won a Whitney Houston lookalike contest, the only other instance in which their names are ever likely to appear in the same sentence is in a list of celebrity Blackburn supporters. And at the end of the dismal 1998-99 season how actor Matt Smith, the eleventh incarnation of the Doctor, must have wished he could

ALL THE BALL SKILLS OF YOUR AVERAGE DALEK

have travelled back in time just four years to when his beloved Rovers ruled the roost … instead of having to watch a bunch of no-hopers with all the ball skills of your average Dalek.

For it was in 1995 that steel magnate Jack Walker's millions bought Rovers the Premiership title – the club's first major trophy since 1928. It is said that star striker Alan Shearer celebrated the title triumph not in a nightclub with scantily clad women, but by creosoting his garden fence. Aye, they know how to have a good time in Blackburn.

But things had changed in those intervening four years. Shearer had gone to

⚽ ODDBALL

FOLLOWING THE INTRODUCTION OF RED CARDS FOR SENDING-OFF OFFENCES IN BRITAIN, BLACKBURN WINGER DAVE WAGSTAFFE HAD THE DUBIOUS DISTINCTION OF BEING THE FIRST PLAYER TO SEE RED WHEN HE WAS DISMISSED AT ORIENT ON 2 OCTOBER 1976.

Newcastle prior to a career on *Match of the Day* where, instead of creosoting the fence, he usually sits on it. Meanwhile Roy Hodgson had moved from managing Inter Milan to take charge at Blackburn – a culture shock on a par with Sophia Loren pulling pints at the Rover's Return. Hodgson had steered Blackburn to a respectable sixth in 1997-98, qualifying for the UEFA Cup to boot, and in the

Manager Roy Hodgson can't hold on to the ball ... or his job.

close season had recruited striker Kevin Davies from Southampton for £7.5 million. Davies repaid Hodgson's faith by failing to score in his first fifteen games for the club. He must have felt like disappearing down one of the town's 4,000 holes. With an early exit in Europe and just two League wins by mid-November, Hodgson was sacked hours after a 2-0 home defeat to bottom club Southampton.

Brian Kidd replaced him, but a 3-1 victory over Wimbledon in March merely delayed the final act. Not even an emotional plea from Walker ahead of a crunch clash could save Rovers, and with no wins from their final eight matches, relegation was confirmed when they failed to beat Kidd's old club, Manchester United, at Ewood Park.

As three disgruntled Rovers fans dissected the season in their local pub, the first moaned: 'Things couldn't get much worse.'

'They could,' said the second fan. 'Jack Walker could pull out and we could be run by a firm of black pudding manufacturers!'

'Or by a bunch of Indian chicken farmers!' laughed the third.

'Don't be so bloody ridiculous!' snapped the other two.

NOTTINGHAM FOREST

1998-99

- ☺ **League: 20th (Premiership)**
- ☺ **FA Cup: 0-1 Portsmouth, round 3**
- ☺ **League Cup: 1-2 Manchester United, round 4**

Whereas Brian Clough succeeded in making a silk purse out of a sow's ear, his successors barely mustered a packet of bacon crisps between them. Their cause was not helped by the unrealistic expectations of Forest fans, who thought their club still had a divine right to be in Europe with a team that was often barely the best in Nottingham. By 1998 Forest's only hope of getting into Europe was to sign Judith Chalmers.

The season was doomed before it started with Forest's star player, petulant Dutch striker Pierre van Hooijdonk, refusing to train with the club because he thought his teammates weren't good enough for the Premiership. He may have been a pain, but he was a shrewd judge of ability. While he went on strike, the rest of the team played as if they had come out in sympathy. Although van Hooijdonk did eventually play a few games, his piqued teammates refused to hug or kiss him when he scored. Definitely no tongues. Fielding a clutch of cut-price foreign imports such as Jean-Claude Darcheville, Jesper Mattsson, Hugo Porfirio and Stale Stensaas, Forest continued to struggle and

A CLUTCH OF CUT-PRICE FOREIGN IMPORTS

Pierre van Hooijdonk (airborne) was about as popular among Forest players as a mumps epidemic.

beleaguered boss Dave Bassett was sacked in January.

Ron Atkinson was put in charge until the end of the season and marked his first home game by going to the wrong dugout. Further proof that he had lost his way came when he paid £1.1m to make Carlton Palmer his first signing. The highlight of Big Ron's reign was an 8-1 home defeat by Manchester United, which he described tongue-in-cheek as 'a nine-goal thriller'. When Forest finished bottom of the table, he announced his retirement from management to concentrate on what used to be called his media career. The board reacted by naming David Platt as the new manager. The Forest faithful will always be grateful to Platt. For without him they would never have had the chance to witness the three hapless Italians – Salvatore Matrecano, Moreno Mannini and Gianluca Petrachi. Their signings rekindled memories of a previous Forest Italian import, Andrea Silenzi, a man described as an old-fashioned centre-forward. And in truth he was almost as good as Nat Lofthouse. But then Nat Lofthouse was seventy-one at the time.

☻ ODDBALL

AFTER HIS OWN-GOAL HAD SEEN NOTTINGHAM FOREST PROMOTED TO DIVISION ONE IN 1977, MILLWALL'S JON MOORE WAS VOTED PLAYER OF THE YEAR BY GRATEFUL FOREST SUPPORTERS.

GLASGOW CELTIC

1999-2000

- ⚽ **League: 2nd (Scottish Premier)**
- ⚽ **Scottish FA Cup: 1-3 Inverness Caledonian Thistle, round 3**
- ⚽ **Scottish League Cup: Winners**
- ⚽ **UEFA Cup: 0-2 (aggregate) Olympique Lyon, round 2**

With Celtic in ailing health, it was decided that the team required urgent medical attention. Of course the club could have brought in Alan Ball to perform the last rites but instead they hoped that Czech coach Dr Jozef Venglos might be able to come up with a cure … despite the fact that he had previously failed to bring about any discernible improvement in the

THE TEAM REQUIRED URGENT MEDICAL ATTENTION

condition of Aston Villa. In his sole year in charge at Celtic Park, Rangers won the treble. Dr Jo became Dr No. Celtic gently eased him aside in the summer of 1999 and in his place unveiled what they hoped would become their Dream Team – the personable, media-friendly John Barnes in his first managerial post, with the taciturn but vastly experienced Kenny Dalglish as technical director of football.

Go into a football club and anyone can instantly tell you what the kit man does, what the secretary does and so on. Yet nobody has the faintest idea what a well-paid technical director does, often least of all the man himself. The post is soccer's

'Technical director' Kenny Dalglish. You'd have that glint in your eye and the dimple in your cheek if you had his job – and his salary.

version of the consultant. Many cynics expressed their own ideas about Dalglish's interpretation of the role, usually involving the perfection of his golf game.

It was clear from the outset that Barnes was in sole charge of team affairs – but he was an eager Boy Scout trying to run a multinational company. The job, as it was

for Gareth Gates with Jordan, was simply too big for him. Quite apart from the traditional early exit in Europe, results were disappointing, coming to a head in February with a humiliating home defeat in the Cup to little Inverness Caledonian Thistle – a result that prompted the classic headline: SUPER CALEY GO BALLISTIC – CELTIC ARE ATROCIOUS. With Dalglish taking over as Mary Poppins until the end of the season, Barnes was hastily ushered out of the door, his chief legacy to football thus remaining the 'Anfield Rap'.

☺ ODDBALL

CELTIC FANS WHO SAT DOWN TO WATCH TV HIGHLIGHTS OF THEIR TEAM'S 7-1 THRASHING OF RANGERS IN THE 1957 SCOTTISH LEAGUE CUP FINAL WERE ABLE TO SEE ONLY THE FIRST HALF – BECAUSE THE CAMERAMAN HAD FORGOTTEN TO REMOVE THE LENS CAP AFTER THE HALF-TIME BREAK.

Germany
2000 EUROPEAN CHAMPIONSHIPS FINALS

There wasn't much for Kevin Keegan's England to smile about at Euro 2000. It was the usual story of being outsmarted by players who were considered barely fit enough to lace the England stars' drinks. But in the depths of despair at another early exit, there was one unlikely consolation: the Germans were even worse. Everyone admires German efficiency – except in the sporting arena. Quite simply, they are too good at too many sports and don't seem to have grasped the British concept of heroic failure. Losing is as alien to a German as foreplay is to an Australian. Cliff Richard was still a young one and Gerry didn't need a pacemaker the last time England had beaten the Germans in a meaningful encounter, so the chance to settle old scores was eagerly anticipated.

Going into Euro 2000, the word on the streets was that the Germans were nothing exceptional. The appointment of coach Erich Ribbeck had been criticized because he was never an international player, and striker Oliver Bierhoff – hero of Euro '96 – had openly questioned his squad selection. But we had

THE GERMANS REALLY WERE CRAP

APPROPRIATELY NAMED GERMAN MIDFIELDER STEFAN EFFENBERG WAS SENT HOME FROM THE 1994 WORLD CUP FINALS AFTER GIVING GERMAN FANS THE FINGER DURING HIS COUNTRY'S UNCONVINCING VICTORY OVER SOUTH KOREA.

heard it all before. How many times had we been told that the Germans weren't as good as usual, only for them to be battling through to the latter stages of a tournament long after our pampered Premiership stars had landed back at Heathrow? But this time was different: the Germans really were crap. Combative goalkeeper Oliver Kahn, who

Lothar Matthäus was running in only one direction: home.

always looked likely to undergo a dramatic transformation when there was a full moon, was constantly complaining about a lack of protection. If only his mother had voiced similar thoughts … In the middle, Lothar Matthäus tried valiantly to defy the march of time but any attack that relied heavily on the lumbering Carsten Jancker was destined to struggle. Jancker – Germany's answer to Emile Heskey – was later said to have been looking for a move to a London club, presumably unaware that he was already part of Cockney rhyming slang.

After drawing with Romania in their opening group game, Germany succumbed to an Alan Shearer goal in the one that mattered. Portugal, having already qualified, then fielded nine reserves but still humbled the Germans 3-0. The highlight was the second goal, Kahn allowing a soft shot from Sergio Conceição to slip under his body. The laughter could be heard all the way back to Jens Lehmann's house. Germany finished bottom of the group, the first time for sixteen years that they had failed to progress beyond the first stage. Now they knew what the rest of us had to put up with.

MIDDLESBROUGH

2000-01

- ☻ **League: 14th (Premiership)**
- ☻ **FA Cup: 1-3 Wimbledon, round 4 replay**
- ☻ **League Cup: 0-1 Wimbledon, round 3**

To some clubs a massive cash injection means being able to paint the crush barriers. To Middlesbrough in the 1990s, chairman Steve Gibson's millions transformed the club from near bankruptcy to a position where they could afford to sign the best players in the world. The man entrusted with spending Gibson's cash wisely was Bryan Robson. Some think Gibson would have earned a better return for his money by investing in Betamax. Over a six-year period Robson attracted star names to

IT WAS LIKE WATCHING ASTROTURF GROW

Teesside, many labouring under the misapprehension that Redcar beach was the next best thing to the Copacabana. Once they got a whiff of their new surroundings, some got straight on to their agent … and then their travel agent. So the brochure was changed to call the new ground the Riverside Stadium, but attempts to portray it as a *Wind in the Willows* setting proved equally unsuccessful. 'Ratty and Mole Visit the Chemical Works' was never high on Kenneth Grahame's agenda.

With little continuity, the limit of Robson's ambition seemed to be to avoid a second relegation. He answered his critics by pointing out that he had put

Middlesbrough on the map. And Jack the Ripper put Whitechapel on the map.

For the 2000-01 season Robson had assembled another expensive squad, including Ugo Ehiogu, Paul Ince and Alen Boksic. By winter results were so bad that Robson wore the haunted look of a politician on *Newsnight* who has just been told that Kirsty Wark is on holiday. With the fans on Robson's back, Gibson sent for Terry Venables to help out the under-fire manager.

Calling in Venables to solve a crisis is a bit like pouring water on a chip-pan fire, but it is an indication of how desperate things were that even he couldn't fail to bring about a marked improvement. By organizing things at the back he made Middlesbrough hard to beat … and even harder to watch. It was like watching Astroturf grow.

In the end, fourteenth place was a decent finish for Middlesbrough fans. And there was better news on the way: Gibson was looking for a new manager.

⚽ ODDBALL

A TEENAGE MIDDLESBROUGH FAN TRIED TO GET ROUND A COURT CURFEW BY WEARING A GORILLA SUIT TO A 1992 LEAGUE CUP TIE AGAINST PETERBOROUGH. BUT WHEN HIS TEAM SCORED, HE THREW THE HEAD INTO THE AIR IN CELEBRATION AND WAS LATER SPOTTED BY A VIGILANT POLICE OFFICER WHO WAS WATCHING THE HIGHLIGHTS ON TV.

Alen Boksic: at least Robson's expensive Boro rose above Bradford City. On this occasion.

LEICESTER CITY

2001-02

- ☺ **League: 20th (Premiership)**
- ☺ **FA Cup: 0-1 West Brom, round 4**
- ☺ **League Cup: 0-6 Leeds United, round 3**

As any football supporter will confirm, the close season is usually a time for unwarranted optimism. No matter how badly your team played the previous season or how dismal your new signings (if any), once the fixtures come out at the end of June reality gives way to dreams. Even East Stirling fans can picture picking up the odd draw before the end of November. But when you lose your first game of the season 5-0 at home to Bolton, the omens are so bad that Mr Micawber would have struggled to put on a brave face. This was the grim scenario that faced Leicester supporters in August 2001 – and just to prove that the Bolton result was no fluke, City crashed 4-0 at Highbury in their next game. Manager Peter Taylor was already under fire for spending £25 million on a string of signings that were an even bigger mystery than how Shaun Wright-Phillips has come to win over thirty England caps. The regular fall guy was £5 million striker Ade Akinbiyi who looked about as comfortable in the Premiership as Roy Cropper at the wheel of a McLaren. After those opening two hammerings goalkeeper Tim Flowers lost his place to Ian Walker, but soon Taylor needed

A GRIM SCENARIO FACED LEICESTER SUPPORTERS

⚽ ODDBALL

TWO LEICESTER PLAYERS – STAN MILBURN AND JACK FROGGATT – COMBINED TO PRODUCE SOCCER'S ONLY INSTANCE OF A SHARED OWN-GOAL. PLAYING AGAINST CHELSEA IN DECEMBER 1954, THE PAIR LUNGED AT THE BALL IN AN ATTEMPT TO CLEAR AND CONNECTED SIMULTANEOUSLY TO SEND IT FLYING INTO THEIR OWN NET.

snookers and it came as no surprise when he was relieved of his duties a little over a month into the season – with Leicester planted at the foot of the table and sending out roots.

Dave Bassett took over and moulded Taylor's team in his own image – experienced, competitive, but limited. With Robbie Savage, Dennis Wise and Frank Sinclair, the side packed a bite that a piranha would have been proud of but only Muzzy Izzet exuded class. Leicester were bottom on Boxing Day and, in a world of few certainties, just about the surest was that they would stay there for the rest of the season. By the end Akinbiyi weighed in with just two goals from sixteen starts, leaving veteran Brian Deane as top scorer with six. In April, just before relegation was confirmed, Bassett was moved upstairs to become director of football, his number two, Micky Adams, taking over as manager to plot the return journey. And so Leicester's last season at Filbert Street, their home since 1891, ended in despair, despite the players managing to rouse themselves for the final game at the old ground, beating Spurs 2-1 to record only their fifth Premiership victory of the campaign. Nevertheless, that summer City fans were confident of bouncing straight back. And for once they were right – although their joy would be as fleeting as a Gordon Brown smile.

Class apart: Muzzy Izzet, a rose among thorns, yet none of those with points enough to save the team from relegation.

France
2002 WORLD CUP FINALS

National supporters react in different ways to exits from major soccer tournaments. In England the mentally challenged choose to riot in small provincial towns that are hotbeds of bowls rather than football; in Italy they throw insults and tomatoes at the players; and in France they simply shrug their shoulders and return to their wine. As the reigning world and European champions France were hot favourites in South Korea and Japan but a stuttering warm-up campaign indicated that maybe all was not well with Roger Lemerre's men. Suddenly their famous 'va va voom' was beginning to sound more like the engine of a Skoda being started on a frosty morning. Robert Pires was already ruled out with injury and, worse still, the world's most accomplished footballer, Zinedine Zidane, injured his left thigh in the warm-up match with South Korea, as a result of which he missed the first two games of the finals. Nevertheless Lemerre was still able to call on world-class performers … and Frank Leboeuf.

ZIDANE WAS WHEELED OUT BUT HE WAS A PALE IMITATION OF HIS NORMAL SELF

The opening match saw France pitted against unfancied Senegal, who were making their first appearance in the finals. Beforehand, the Africans pinpointed Leboeuf as France's weakest link and so it proved as his ageing legs struggled to keep pace with the speedy Senegalese forwards. It was like watching Dixon of Dock Green chasing two teenage muggers. And when a mix-up between Emmanuel Petit and the ever eccentric Fabien Barthez gifted Papa Bouba Diop the only goal of the game, Senegal had pulled off the biggest shock in world football since Steve McManaman was seen breaking into a sweat. The only good news for the French was that Leboeuf had joined the injury list.

Their next opponents were Uruguay but the game ended in a disappointing goalless draw, France suffering a further blow when Thierry Henry was sent off in the first half for a bad tackle. It was his only contribution to the tournament. Without Henry France now needed to beat Denmark in their final group game. Zidane was wheeled out, his left thigh heavily strapped, but he was a pale imitation of his normal self and the Danes won 2-0. John Motson probably told us that it was

⚽ ODDBALL

AT THE START OF A FRENCH CLUB MATCH IN 1950 ONE OF THE CAPTAINS ACCIDENTALLY SWALLOWED THE FIVE-FRANC PIECE WHICH THE REFEREE WAS TOSSING FOR CHOICE OF ENDS.

the first time France had lost a competitive fixture with Zidane in the side since he made his international debut in 1994. France thus became the first reigning champions to be knocked out at the opening stage of a World Cup tournament since Brazil in 1966. Before Lemerre's inevitable sacking the French camp said there were no excuses for their lamentable displays … apart from injuries, bad luck – and unsatisfactory croissants at the team hotel. Sent home without a win or even a goal to their name, the players might have expected a rough ride on their return to Paris. But on the Champs Elysées fans simply gave a familiar Gallic shrug.

Early exit: Zinedine Zidane holds his head, France no longer hold the World Cup.

ASTON VILLA

2002-03

- ☺ **League: 16th (Premiership)**
- ☺ **FA Cup: 1-4 Blackburn, round 3**
- ☺ **League Cup: 3-4 Liverpool, round 5**

It was on 16 September 2002 that Villa fans knew this would be a season to forget. That Monday evening, during a fiercely contested Birmingham derby at St Andrew's, Villa's Finnish goalkeeper Peter Enckelman allowed an Olof Mellberg throw-in to squirm under his foot and into the net. It was a blunder that would have made Abi Titmuss blush. Birmingham went on to complete the double over their great rivals, ensuring that Villa fans had even less to cheer about than usual. For if Chelsea, Arsenal and Manchester United are the stylish suits of the Premier League, for years Villa were the beige cardigan. They rarely strayed far from mid-table, with the result that their season usually started to wind down the day after the third round of the FA Cup. A goal was such a rarity that it was greeted with the same hysteria accorded an English name on the Arsenal team sheet. Quite simply, Villa were duller than a Nigel Mansell victory speech.

VILLA ARE DULLER THAN A NIGEL MANSELL VICTORY SPEECH

Chairman Doug Ellis – only Rome wasn't sacked by Deadly Doug – was renowned for keeping a tight grip on the purse strings. Captain Hook is the only person to have put his hands in his pockets less. Rumour had it that even as

✪ ODDBALL

VILLA STRIKER SAVO MILOSEVIC WAS TRANSFER-LISTED IN 1998 AFTER SPITTING AT HIS OWN FANS DURING A DEFEAT AT BLACKBURN.

late as 2003 the club's transfer kitty contained pound notes. Indeed, critics said that prising transfer funds from Ellis was football's equivalent of a Mick Jagger paternity suit: like getting blood out of a Stone. Given this perceived lack of ambition – Doug called it 'prudent housekeeping' – Villa sometimes struggled to attract top managers. But even the fans were shocked in 2002 when Graham Taylor swapped his role on the board for a second stint in charge.

Taylor has always had a fondness for beanpole strikers. In his first spell he utilized Ian Ormondroyd, who was more of a danger to planes taking off from Birmingham International Airport than he was to the

opposition goal. This time Taylor gave the lanky Peter Crouch fourteen games. He proved equally effective, failing to hit the target once. There *were* good strikers at Villa Park, but mostly in visiting teams. In the Cup old boy Dwight Yorke scored twice for Blackburn to silence the Holte End, not that it needed much that season. By January Villa had scored just four goals in ten away League games before pulling off a 5-2 win at Middlesbrough. Normal service was quickly resumed, however. At the back Villa were reasonably solid. Steve Staunton was like a steamroller – with acceleration to match – and, although they flirted with relegation, it never reached the heavy petting stage. That would have been too much like excitement.

Look back in anguish: Aston Villa's Enckelman takes in the horror of his gaffe against Birmingham City and puts his head in his hands. It's a wonder he didn't drop it.

LIVERPOOL

2002-03

- League: 5th (Premiership)
- FA Cup: 0-2 Crystal Palace, round 4 replay
- League Cup: Winners
- Europe: Champions League exit at first stage
- UEFA Cup: 1-3 (aggregate) Celtic, quarter-final

Whereas Anfield was once a fortress, in 2002-03 the Big Bad Asthmatic Wolf could have blown Liverpool's house down. They won fewer than half their home games in the League while in Cup competitions they suffered embarrassing Anfield defeats to Crystal Palace and Celtic. There were even calls for Jimmy Corkhill to take over as manager. Yet Gérard Houllier's men had started solidly, staying unbeaten in their first dozen League games, but after a 1-0 defeat at Middlesbrough in November the rot set in. Still, as long as El Hadji Diouf was in the side, they remained within spitting distance of the leaders. The trouble was that Diouf and the other new summer signings, fellow Senegalese Salif Diao and French import Bruno Cheyrou, proved big disappointments. Their failure to deliver was worthy of the Royal Mail. Meanwhile the centre of defence was so slow it was declared a pedestrian zone, and in goal Jerzy Dudek's handling evoked comparisons with Heathrow baggage staff

THEIR FAILURE TO DELIVER WAS WORTHY OF THE ROYAL MAIL

One for the album: Emile Heskey shows strength and determination.

on the night flight to Malaga. So it was a good job Liverpool could rely on the goals of Emile Heskey – all six of them. This was the season when Virgin Atlantic named two new planes after the Liverpool strikers. One plane was named Michael Owen because it was fast and direct; the other was named Emile Heskey because it had a turning circle of ten minutes.

A team containing Steven Gerrard and Owen should have been major contenders but Houllier had, for the most part, surrounded his two genuine artists with a bunch of cowboy decorators. The upshot was that Liverpool were knocked out of the FA Cup early, Europe twice and finished nineteen points behind their friends from Old Trafford, fifth place meaning that they failed to qualify for the following season's Champions League. All they had to show for a season that had promised much was the worthless Worthington Cup. They couldn't even

⚽ ODDBALL

ROBBIE FOWLER WAS ONCE SIDELINED FROM THE LIVERPOOL TEAM WITH A KNEE INJURY AFTER HE STRETCHED TO PICK UP HIS TV REMOTE CONTROL.

complete their Panini stickers album: Dudek was missing. Nothing new there then.

Scotland
2002-04

Let's face it, the union of Scotland and Berti Vogts was the unlikeliest since John Major and Edwina Currie. The little chap had excellent credentials, having coached Germany to the Euro '96 title, but the general feeling was that the Scottish FA didn't need a foreign coach to make a mess of things – they were doing a perfectly good job of that them-selves. If Berti's early results with Scotland scarcely suggested that he was the nation's Messiah, his growing army of critics had a field day when his new charges opened their Euro 2004 qualifiers against the Faeroe Islands,

THE WORST SCOTTISH PERFORMANCE IN 130 YEARS

the footballing equivalent of the amoeba.

After thirteen minutes the Scots were two goals down, thanks to a level of organization not seen since the Keystone Cops. Although they fought back for a draw, the press labelled it the worst performance in 130 years of Scottish football. The *Scotsman* wrote witheringly: 'David Weir and Christian Dailly gave a demonstration of the art of the central defender of which Ally McCoist would have been ashamed.' Thereafter Berti's name rarely appeared in the Scottish press without the prefix 'bumbling'.

Scotland's Paul Dickov has the can-can down to a fine art but the football, as the Faeroe Islands discovered to their joy in this match in 2002, was a bit more slipshod.

With Berti continuing to hand out international caps like sweeties, Scotland blundered their way through the group before crashing out 6-1 on aggregate to Holland in a play-off. The finals in Portugal would be for the grown-ups. In February 2004 Berti's men were on the receiving end of a 4-0 friendly drubbing by Wales, which is roughly on a par with a professional boxer being knocked out by Jarvis Cocker.

With Berti's reputation in tatters, a good start to the 2006 World Cup qualifiers was essential but his tactics remained harder to fathom than a Garth Crooks question. Instead Scotland picked up just two points from three games – scrambled draws against Slovenia and Moldova – at which point Berti quit after two-and-a-half years in charge. He said he had resigned because the supporters clearly wanted him out. It was one of the few things he got right. In some ways Berti Vogts would

⚽ ODDBALL

FOLLOWING A VIOLENT MATCH WITH RANGERS IN 1988, HEARTS DIRECTOR DOUGLAS PARK LOCKED SCOTTISH REFEREE DAVID SYME IN HIS DRESSING ROOM AND HID THE KEY.

be a tough act to follow ... but then so was Richard Nixon.

EVERTON

2003-04

- ⊕ **League: 17th (Premiership)**
- ⊕ **FA Cup: 1-2 Fulham, round 4**
- ⊕ **League Cup: 4-5 (on penalties) Middlesbrough, round 4**

This was the season when Everton were supposed to become a force in the land once more. They had a bright young manager in David Moyes and in his first year in charge he had led them to a highly respectable finishing place of seventh. And they had the Boy Wonder, Wayne Rooney, the most exciting young talent in English football. Some fans were barely old enough for their first ASBO the last time there was this much optimism around Goodison Park.

THE SEASON PROVED A MASSIVE ANTI-CLIMAX

At times Rooney has played like Gary Lineker, Kevin Keegan and Michael Owen all rolled into one. But for him and girlfriend Coleen – the council-house Posh and Becks – the season proved a massive anti-climax. Rooney couldn't buy a goal (and Coleen must have tried), ending up with just nine to his name in the League. Even Rooney's grandmother could have put away some of the chances he missed. This would not be the last time the words 'Rooney' and 'grandmother' would be used in the same sentence. Without his input Everton never lived up to expectations. Goals were in short supply throughout and the team closed the season with just one

Everton's Lee Carsley does sit-ups in punishment for being part of such a crap team while Rooney looks on and dreams of transfers.

win in ten games, culminating in a five-goal thumping at Manchester City. Their total of thirty-nine points was Everton's lowest for over a hundred years, but was just enough to enable them to cling to their Premiership status.

After defeat to lowly Wolves a furious Moyes raged at the players and cancelled their golf social. Almost overnight the new Alex Ferguson had become the new Ally MacLeod. There were dark mutterings that Moyes had lost the dressing room – something that Cloughie probably did at Forest in a tired and emotional moment. But what a difference a summer made. Rooney moved on to pastures new and a new mellow Moyes emerged, kinder to the skin. Everyone was happy. Moyes had a willing, energetic new team, Rooney had got his dream move to Manchester and Coleen had enough money to buy all the clothes she'll ever need … and with a little left over for a good divorce lawyer if necessary.

⊛ ODDBALL

TWICE IN THE SPACE OF FOUR DAYS IN MARCH 1972 EVERTON DEFENDER TOMMY WRIGHT SCORED OWN-GOALS INSIDE THE FIRST MINUTE, FIRST AGAINST LIVERPOOL AND THEN AGAINST MANCHESTER UNITED.

LEEDS UNITED

2003-04

- League: 19th (Premiership)
- FA Cup: 1-4 Arsenal, round 3
- League Cup: 2-3 Manchester United, round 3

There are some hard jobs in football – refereeing a Milan derby; drawing up a five-year plan to get Halifax Town into the Premiership; acting as Craig Bellamy's public relations advisor – but managing Leeds United in the early twenty-first century must rank as one of the toughest. Leeds paid the price for the extravagance of former chairman Peter Ridsdale, whose spending spree made Elton John look like Scrooge. Among his purchases were eleven tropical fish in the Leeds colours of blue, yellow and white. Presumably if he had been chairman of Newcastle he would have bought a herd of zebras to graze on the pitch. Arguably his greatest extravagance was hiring Terry Venables in July 2002. Venables wasted no time in splashing out £2.75m on old chum Nick Barmby (Terry Fenwick must have been on holiday). Predictably the love affair between Ridsdale and Venables soon ended in a messy break-up in March 2003 and Peter Reid was brought in to turn things round and stave off relegation. But Elland Road was like DFS – every day a sale. Rio Ferdinand, Jonathan Woodgate and

ELLAND ROAD WAS LIKE DFS – EVERY DAY A SALE

Harry Kewell had all been sold to balance the books, leaving Reid to start the 2003-04 season with a squad so thin it was positively anorexic.

Reid made two grave errors that alienated the fans. One was dispensing with the services of his assistant, Eddie Gray, who had been at Leeds so long he could remember when Norman Hunter bit rusks rather than legs. The other was signing Brazilian World Cup winning defender Roque Junior. Taken on a one-year loan from AC Milan, Roque Junior was brushed aside by opposing strikers like an irritating flake of dandruff. He barely appeared to have the physique and resolve to cope with a Friday evening trip around Sainsbury's, let alone deal with the best forwards in the Premiership. He played only five League games and the Leeds faithful were mightily relieved when he returned from international duty with an Achilles injury, as a result of which he was sent back to Italy in January 2004. By then Reid had been sacked, with Leeds bottom of the table following a 6-1 thrashing at Portsmouth.

In a comeback worthy of Lazarus, Gray was appointed caretaker manager. Although still able to call upon the services of Alan Smith and Mark Viduka, Gray could not keep Leeds up. It would be second-tier football at Elland Road, with the only bright spot being that Barmby was on the road to Hull.

⚽ **ODDBALL**

FORMER LEEDS FULLBACK WILLIE BELL RESIGNED FROM HIS JOB AS LINCOLN CITY MANAGER IN 1978 TO JOIN A RELIGIOUS SECT IN AMERICA.

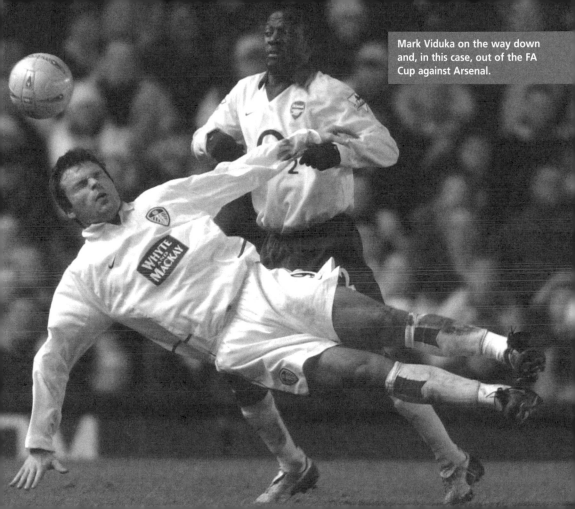

Mark Viduka on the way down and, in this case, out of the FA Cup against Arsenal.

Northern Ireland
2004 EUROPEAN CHAMPIONSHIPS QUALIFIERS

Northern Ireland have always been the caramel cup in the great chocolate box of European football – colourless, unfancied and really there only to make up the numbers. Apart from reaching the World Cup finals in 1958 and 1982 (optimism rears its ugly head once every quarter-century), Northern Ireland's history has been a catalogue of unremitting failure. Their lack of success has been comparable to that of Albania in the Eurovision Song Contest. But even by Northern Ireland standards their qualifying group for Euro 2004 was particularly dire. It would be the nation's Waterloo – although the quality was more Boom-Bang-a-Bang.

A CATALOGUE OF UNREMITTING FAILURE

Between February 2002, when Steve Lomas scored against Poland, and February 2004, when David Healy was on the mark in a 4-1 defeat to Norway, Northern Ireland went a record 1,298 minutes without a goal. A one-eyed fisherman would have been more adept at finding the net. During that drought they failed to breach such flimsy defences as Liechtenstein, Cyprus and Armenia and plunged to 124th in the

⚽ ODDBALL

MAKING HIS LEAGUE DEBUT FOR BARNET IN 1995, NORTHERN IRELAND KEEPER MAIK TAYLOR WAS BEATEN BY AN 80-YARD DROP KICK FROM HIS OPPOSITE NUMBER, HEREFORD UNITED'S CHRIS MACKENZIE.

FIFA world rankings – just below St Winifred's Girls' School Choir. Under manager Sammy McIlroy their eight qualifying group matches had one common factor – the word 'nil'. There seemed a better chance of Ian Paisley and Gerry Adams going out clubbing together than Northern Ireland ever scoring another goal.

After defeat to Greece in the final qualifier in October 2003 extended Northern Ireland's scoreless run to thirteen games, McIlroy quit to become manager of Stockport County, who were then lurking dangerously close to the bottom of Division Two. Evidence that the strain had got to him came when he declared: 'Stockport have great ambition and potential.' Here was a man in need of a rest.

His successor, Lawrie Sanchez, broke the hoodoo in his first game in charge, thanks to Healy's goal, and, when Estonia were beaten 1-0 in a friendly at the end of March 2004, it was Northern Ireland's first win for nearly two-and-a-half years. They may not have reached orange cream status but at least they had made it up to hazelnut whirl.

Northern Ireland play so poorly even their manager can't bear to watch. Beleaguered Sammy McIlroy hangs his head in shame as Armenia thrash his boys.

SOUTHAMPTON

2004-05

- ☺ **League: 20th (Premiership)**
- ☺ **FA Cup: 0-4 Manchester United, round 6**
- ☺ **League Cup: 2-5 Watford, round 4**

It didn't need Mystic Meg to predict troubled times ahead for Southampton when they sacked manager Paul Sturrock two games into the new season. One of the reasons cited for his abrupt exit was his poor dress sense, which apparently upset certain members of the board. While Sturrock may not have been catwalk material, there wasn't exactly a rush to recruit Martin Jol as the next James Bond or to put Arsène Wenger on *Celebrity Love Island*. Saints' ex-public schoolboy chairman Rupert Lowe

REDKNAPP AND ASSISTANT JIM SMITH WERE NO MIRACLE WORKERS

replaced Sturrock with Steve Wigley who, although lacking any previous managerial experience, at least gave the impression that his wardrobe contained a suit. But by December a string of desperate results – including a League Cup trouncing at Watford – led Rupert to appoint tie-wearing Harry Redknapp as the club's twelfth manager in ten years.

To call Redknapp's appointment 'controversial' would be like describing Rik Waller as 'a bit chubby', for two weeks earlier Redknapp had resigned from Portsmouth and publicly stated that he would not be joining their bitter rivals. Pompey fans were baying for blood.

Their mood lightened somewhat when it became apparent that Redknapp and assistant Jim Smith (the Muttley to his Dick Dastardly) were no miracle workers. Southampton continued to hover in or around the relegation zone, their cause not helped when midfielder David Prutton picked up a ten-match ban for manhandling referee Alan Wiley. Quite what Mr Wiley had done to provoke such an uncharacteristic tantrum remains open to speculation – but rumour has it that he had threatened to ruffle Prutton's immaculately coiffed hair. And under Rupert's regime a hair out of place or a split end was punished by a fine of a week's wages. Dandruff brought about immediate termination of contract.

A four-goal drubbing at Portsmouth – where goalkeeper Antti Niemi played more like Harry's Auntie Naomi – hastened the decline and, when Southampton lost at home to Manchester United on the last day,

⚽ ODDBALL

WHEN HE WAS SOUTHAMPTON MANAGER GRAEME SOUNESS RECEIVED A CALL HE THOUGHT WAS FROM WORLD FOOTBALLER OF THE YEAR GEORGE WEAH, RECOMMENDING THIRTY-ONE-YEAR-OLD SENEGAL STRIKER ALI DIA. SOUNESS GAVE THE UNKNOWN A FIRST-TEAM GAME BUT SOON REALIZED HE HAD BEEN CONNED. THE CALL WAS A HOAX. AFTER A PREMIERSHIP CAREER LASTING JUST FIFTY-THREE MINUTES, ALI DIA WAS SHIPPED OFF TO SOMEWHERE NEARER HIS TRUE STANDARD – GATESHEAD.

they slid out of the top flight for the first time in twenty-seven years.

Still, as Rupert pointed out in his programme notes for that game, all was not doom and gloom. The club's radio station, catering facilities and shop were all flourishing, the latter presumably doing a nice line in red-and-white gents' blazers. It seemed only a matter of time before Rupert unveiled Laurence Llewelyn-Bowen as manager.

Southampton manager Harry Redknapp: no miracle worker.

WOLVERHAMPTON WANDERERS

2004-05

- League: 9th (Championship)
- FA Cup: 0-2 Arsenal, round 4
- League Cup: 2-4 (penalties) Burnley after 1-1 draw, round 2

Being crap is relative. Just ask Jedward. So whilst the Wolves class of 2004-05 were desperate underachievers, they were almost a success compared with the Molineux teams of the 1980s, which plunged from the First Division to the Fourth in just three years. The difference was that eighties Wolves were in dire straits financially; noughties Wolves were bankrolled by the £160-million-pound man, Sir Jack Hayward.

When Hayward bought Wolves in 1990,

DAVID BLUNKETT WAS BETTER AT HOLDING ON TO A LEAD THAN WOLVES

he promised to throw millions at the club 'until the men in white coats come to take me away'. His subsequent hiring of first Graham Taylor, then Mark McGhee and Colin Lee to fulfil his dreams suggested that the men in white coats were on standby at the very least. Finally, in 2003, Dave Jones earned Wolves promotion to the Premiership – but like all the best dreams, it didn't last long enough because of an inability to keep a clean sheet.

Relegated to the Championship, Wolves were expected to bounce straight back, but a poor start with no wins in their first seven League games left them nineteenth at one stage. Following a 1-0 defeat by ten-man

Although the team lost only one of the final twenty-five matches, they finished seven points outside the play-offs, chiefly because they drew no fewer than twenty-one games. That season, David Blunkett was better at holding on to a lead than Wolves. For, despite the presence of veterans Paul Ince and Colin Cameron in midfield and £3 million Scottish striker Kenny Miller, the side lacked bite. They were sheep in wolves' clothing.

Wolves' dire performance in the 2004-05 season soon wiped the smile off Paul Ince's face.

Gillingham at the end of October, Jones was sacked and replaced by former England boss Glenn Hoddle who, at forty-seven, was still often the best player in training. More worrying was the fact that Eileen Drewery would have been the second best.

⚽ ODDBALL

AMONG WOLVES' SCORERS WHEN THEY BEAT NEWCASTLE 3-1 IN THE 1908 FA CUP FINAL WAS A VICAR. REV. KENNETH HUNT SCORED THEIR FIRST GOAL AGAINST THE MAGPIES TO BECOME THE ONLY CLERGYMAN TO COLLECT AN FA CUP WINNERS' MEDAL. IT IS SAID THAT WHEN HE TOLD HIS TEAMMATES THAT GOD WAS ON THEIR SIDE, THE REFEREE DEMANDED TO KNOW WHY HIS NAME WASN'T ON THE TEAM SHEET.

SUNDERLAND

2005-06

- ⚽ **League: 20th (Premiership)**
- ⚽ **FA Cup: 1-2 Brentford, round 4**
- ⚽ **League Cup: 0-3 Arsenal, round 3**

When Sunderland left Roker Park in 1997 for their new home at the Stadium of Light, they understandably decided to change their nickname from 'the Rokermen'. They eventually chose 'the Black Cats' in the hope that it would bring them luck. Among the rejected ideas was 'the Miners', which would surely have been more appropriate given the regularity with which they went down.

Mick McCarthy had taken Sunderland up the previous season, but the club purse strings were tighter than a camel's arse in a sandstorm. He had just £5 million to spend, £1.8 million of which went on striker Jonathan Stead from Blackburn. Stead finally scored his first – and only – goal of the season at the twenty-seventh attempt in a 2-2 draw with Everton, although the fact that the match took place on 1 April meant that many fans refused to believe that Stead had broken his duck at last. The other new striker, Andy Gray – bought from Sheffield United for £1.1 million – weighed in with just one goal in twenty-two appearances. Together he and Stead fired more blanks than a pair of eunuchs.

By Christmas, Sunderland had fewer

THEY FIRED MORE BLANKS THAN A PAIR OF EUNUCHS

Everton defenders try to keep straight faces as Jonathan Stead rues another miss.

☻ ODDBALL

AT THE END OF THE 1992 FA CUP FINAL, SUNDERLAND, BEATEN 2-0 BY LIVERPOOL, WERE MISTAKENLY GIVEN THE WINNERS' MEDALS WHILE LIVERPOOL WERE HANDED THE RUNNERS-UP MEDALS. THE PLAYERS SWAPPED AFTERWARDS.

points than the Star of David, so it came as no surprise when McCarthy was sacked in March. His temporary replacement was former Sunderland player Kevin Ball, affectionately known as 'the Hatchet' for a style of play that stopped just short of grievous bodily harm. Under Ball, Sunderland picked up five points from a possible thirty, including a 4-1 drubbing at home to Newcastle, their heaviest defeat to their bitter rivals in over fifty years. They finished with a mere fifteen points, breaking their own Premiership record for the lowest points total in a season (nineteen in 2002-03) and only avoiding the stigma of being the first club to go through an entire season without a home victory by winning their last home game – 2-1 in a re-arranged fixture against Fulham. Even that was a close shave, as Sunderland had been trailing in the original game on April 8 when it was abandoned because of snow. For once, fortune favoured the Black Cats.

It turned out that Sunderland had chosen the wrong lucky omen all along. What they really needed to re-establish themselves in the top division was the luck of the Irish – and it came the following season in the shape of new manager Roy Keane and new chairman Niall Quinn, the world's tallest leprechaun.

NOTTINGHAM FOREST

2005-06

- **League: 7th (League 1)**
- **FA Cup: 0-3 Chester City, round 2**
- **League Cup: 2-3 Macclesfield Town, round 1**

In 2004-05, the combined efforts of Joe Kinnear, Mick Harford and Gary Megson ensured that Nottingham Forest became the first European Cup winners ever to fall into their domestic third division. It was a humiliating comedown. For Forest, playing in League 1 was like finding Sir Alan Sugar sleeping rough or Jack Nicklaus reduced to playing a round of crazy golf.

Megson was entrusted with the task of leading the anticipated return to the Championship in 2005-06 but he claimed the team he had inherited was undisciplined and unfit. For other appropriate adjectives to describe the players, he had only to look in the thesaurus under 'utter shite'.

Megson had spent three unhappy months at the City Ground as a player in 1984, but failed to make a single appearance under Brian Clough, who remarked at the time: 'Gary Megson couldn't trap a landmine.' Which begs the question: why did Clough sign him from Sheffield Wednesday? And now history was repeating itself as embarrassing Cup defeats to League 2 opposition, and a playing style that was about as easy on the eye as a pus-filled stye, soon had the Forest fans calling for

A PLAYING STYLE THAT WAS AS EASY ON THE EYE AS A PUS-FILLED STYE

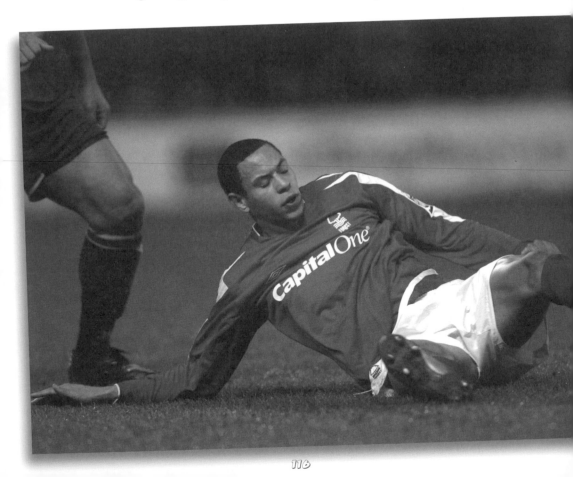

than Tyson hits the ground ... Nottingham Forest hit
ck bottom.

Megson's head. Even by ginger standards he was unpopular.

Despite splashing out a combined £1 million on strikers Nathan Tyson from Wycombe Wanderers and Grant Holt from Rochdale, the slump continued and a run of one win in ten games, culminating in a 3-0 capitulation at Oldham in February, left Forest just four points above the drop zone and led to Megson's departure by 'mutual consent'. After the turmoil and division under Kinnear, Megson had at least united the fans: they all wanted him out.

⚽ ODDBALL

BRIAN CLOUGH'S UNUSUAL TRAINING SESSIONS INCLUDED MAKING THE FOREST SQUAD RUN THROUGH A LARGE PATCH OF STINGING NETTLES AND ORDERING THEM TO SCOUR THE HEDGEROWS FOR MUSHROOMS. ON ANOTHER OCCASION, HE ARRANGED A COMPETITION TO SEE HOW MANY PLAYERS WOULD FIT INTO A FIVE-A-SIDE NET.

LEEDS UNITED

2006-07

- **League: 24th (Championship)**
- **FA Cup: 1-3 West Bromwich Albion, round 3**
- **League Cup: 1-3 Southend United, round 3**

It is fair to say that if you were looking for someone to play Santa Claus, neither Ken Bates (despite the facial resemblance) nor Dennis Wise would exactly be top of the list. Indeed, with their abrasive reputations, they would probably come somewhere below Papa Doc or Albert Steptoe. Yet Ken and Den had been firm friends since their days together at Chelsea and Bates was godfather to Wise's son. So when Bates became chairman of ailing Leeds United in January 2005, it was widely expected that he would make Wise an offer he couldn't refuse to become the club's next manager. Instead, Bates stood by the sitting tenant, Kevin Blackwell, who took Leeds to the 2005-06 Championship play-off final, where they surrendered to Watford with a lack of fight that would even have embarrassed Audley Harrison.

THE VULTURES WERE NOT ONLY CIRCLING, THEY HAD GOT THEIR NAPKINS OUT

Blackwell's first task that summer was jury service, but many Leeds fans had already decided on his guilt following the tame performance in Cardiff. With money from the £2.2 million sale of striker Rob Hulse to Sheffield United, Dave Livermore was signed from Millwall in July. A few days later, another midfielder,

Kevin Nicholls, joined from Luton for £700,000, prompting Blackwell to sell Livermore to Hull after a stay of just ten days at Elland Road. This was a shock: usually it took managers at least two weeks to decide Livermore wasn't worth keeping.

Blackwell knew at the start of the season that the vultures were not only circling, they had actually got their napkins out. So it came as no surprise that when Leeds soon found themselves in the bottom three, Bates gave Blackwell the sack. John Carver was placed in temporary charge, but his five games saw seventeen goals conceded, and in October Wise and his assistant Gus Poyet finally arrived from Swindon. At his first press conference, Wise said he wanted his Leeds to be a little bit nasty, like the Leeds of old. As it transpired, he would have been better advised persuading Charlton, Lorimer, Giles, Hunter and co. to come out of retirement.

⚽ ODDBALL

EAGER TO BEAT THE OTHER TWENTY-SIX CLUBS WHO WANTED TO SIGN FIFTEEN-YEAR-OLD SCOTTISH SENSATION PETER LORIMER IN 1962, LEEDS BOSS DON REVIE WAS IN SUCH A HURRY TO OBTAIN THE SCHOOLBOY'S SIGNATURE THAT HE WAS STOPPED FOR SPEEDING ON HIS WAY TO LORIMER'S HOUSE.

Despite signing a number of experienced players, including ex-Chelsea colleague Tore Andre Flo, Wise was unable to stop the rot. Attendances slumped to around 18,000, and some of those were critical journalists who had to pay for their own tickets after being banned from the press box by Bates. It was one way of raising money. Three successive home wins fostered hopes of a great escape, but late goals conceded at Colchester and Southampton virtually

ensured that Leeds would be playing in the third tier for the first time in their history.

With relegation all but certain, the club – with estimated debts of £35 million – went into administration, incurring a ten-point penalty. While the Football League investigated the circumstances surrounding the club's insolvency, it was suggested that they might also look into whether Leeds had fielded a weakened side – all season.

That season, nobody would have mistaken Dennis Wise's gesture as V for Victory.

DERBY COUNTY

2007-08

- ⊕ **League: 20th (Premiership)**
- ⊕ **FA Cup: 1-4 Preston North End, round 4**
- ⊕ **League Cup: 6-7 (penalties) Blackpool after 2-2 draw, round 2**

Bookmakers aren't renowned for their generosity. Whilst they will happily take your bets on unlikely events such as Elvis being found alive and working in an Indian call centre or the Dalai Lama becoming the next host of *The One Show*, they only pay out on certainties. So when, just five games into the 2007-08 season following a 6-0 mauling by Liverpool, Irish bookmakers Paddy Power decided to pay out on Derby County to be relegated, you knew the club was doomed.

THE PREMIER LEAGUE'S EARLIEST EVER DEMOTION

The Rams were lambs to the slaughter as they went on to muster just one League win all season, lose twenty-nine of their thirty-eight games, and finish with a record low Premier League points total of just eleven. They conceded a staggering eighty-nine goals, letting in six on four occasions and five twice.

Their predicament led pundits to ask: What's the difference between the Derby goalkeeper and a taxi driver? A: A taxi driver only lets in four at a time.

The man in charge at the start of Derby's season from hell was feisty Scot Billy Davies. He had worked wonders to earn Derby promotion in his first season as manager, but paid the price for being successful too soon. The team were clearly ill-equipped for the challenge ahead, not that Davies helped matters by splashing out £3 million on defender Claude Davis, rated by one local commentator as Derby's worst ever major signing. Fans moaned that Davis was a liability when he was in the treatment room and an even bigger one when he was fit.

Derby were no better at the other end of the pitch, failing to find the net between 29 September and 8 December, when in a 4-1 defeat at Old Trafford, Steve Howard finally scored their first away goal – at the ninth attempt. Their leading marksman at the end of the season was Kenny Miller with a measly four League goals. Judging the club's Goal of the Season award must have been like trying to decide which of Simon Cowell, Louis Walsh and Piers Morgan is the least annoying.

Despite his team being firmly rooted to the foot of the table, Davies received a vote of confidence from new chairman Adam Pearson at the end of October. Less than a month later, he was out of a job. His successor Paul Jewell promised: 'I'm not here to wave the white flag. We're not adrift.' He forgot to add the word 'yet'. Shortly before Christmas, there was talk of Derby being taken over by Disney – quite appropriate for a Mickey Mouse team.

Jewell brought in eight players in the January transfer window, including Everton defender Alan Stubbs, Rangers keeper Roy Carroll and Blackburn midfielder Robbie Savage, but it was like trying to plug the leak on the *Titanic* with sticking plaster. Under Jewell, Derby picked up just five points from a possible seventy-two and were officially relegated on 29 March – the Premier League's earliest ever demotion. They finished twenty-four points below the team directly above them, Birmingham City.

Derby's misery was Sunderland's joy. Not

only were the Black Cats delighted that Derby had taken their unwanted record for the lowest points total, but they revelled in the fact that the only club to be beaten by the worst team in Premier League history was Newcastle, defeated 1-0 at Pride Park on 17 September.

⚽ ODDBALL

WHEN DERBY PLAYED EAST MIDLANDS RIVALS NOTTINGHAM FOREST AT PRIDE PARK IN MARCH 2004, A PASS BACK TO FOREST KEEPER BARRY ROCHE HIT A DISCARDED PLASTIC COFFEE CUP AND BOBBLED UP, CAUSING ROCHE TO SLICE THE BALL INTO THE PATH OF DERBY'S PAUL PESCHISOLIDO, WHO FIRED THE BALL INTO THE EMPTY NET. DERBY WENT ON TO WIN 4-2 AND THE COFFEE CUP, SIGNED BY PESCHISOLIDO, NOW SITS IN DERBY'S TROPHY CABINET.

Billy Davies tries to calculate how long he has left before he's sacked.

COVENTRY CITY

2007-08

- ⚽ **League: 21st (Championship)**
- ⚽ **FA Cup: 0-5 West Bromwich Albion, round 5**
- ⚽ **League Cup: 1-2 West Ham United, round 4**

Apart from their FA Cup triumph in 1987, success has been a stranger to Coventry City. Like uninvited guests at a party, they clung resolutely to top-flight status for thirty-four years but the season of 2007-08 – one short of their 125th anniversary – found them languishing in the lower reaches of the Championship. Even lifting the Birmingham Senior Cup for the first time in eighty-four years, courtesy of a thrilling extra-time victory over Walsall, had failed to capture the imagination of the Coventry public. There's just no pleasing some people.

SUCCESS HAS BEEN A STRANGER TO COVENTRY CITY

The manager was Iain Dowie, a man who had entered football folklore for coining the term 'bouncebackability' in his days at Crystal Palace and who has been voted the least photogenic footballer of all time in *The Sun*, beating off stiff competition from the likes of Peter Beardsley, Wayne Rooney and Robert Earnshaw. When *The Guardian* published unflattering photos comparing Dowie to *Doctor Who* monster Davros, it was rumoured that Davros was planning to sue.

The season started promisingly with a 4-1 win at Barnsley and Dowie was named

Michael Mifsud: the one bright spot in a season of misery.

manager of the month for August. Then in September two goals from Maltese forward Michael Mifsud gave the Sky Blues an unlikely 2-0 victory at Old Trafford in the third round of the Carling Cup. However, the following month a transfer embargo was imposed on Coventry after an instalment of striker Leon Best's £650,000 fee was not paid to his previous club, Southampton. The embargo was not lifted until a consortium fronted by former Manchester City defender Ray Ranson bought the cash-strapped club in December – just thirty minutes before it was due to go into administration. Inevitably there was much talk of 'exciting times' and 'a bright future', but Bernard Matthews probably peddled the same lines to his turkeys every November.

As if to prove the point, four straight League losses in January, followed by a 1-0 defeat at the hands of fellow strugglers Preston on 9 February, left City just four points above the drop zone. Dowie was getting stick from the fans. Clearly it was the ugly stick. Dowie was replaced by Chris Coleman, and despite losing 4-1 to Charlton in their final match, Coventry stayed up by a single point at the expense of local rivals Leicester.

Since then managers have come and gone, but by April 2011, Coventry's prospects of rejoining the Premier League party still appeared as remote as Colonel Gaddafi receiving an invitation to the Royal Wedding.

⚽ ODDBALL

MANAGER BOBBY GOULD SIGNED LEFT-BACK STUART PEARCE FOR COVENTRY IN 1983 AFTER WATCHING HIM PLAY FOR WEALDSTONE ON A MISERABLE NIGHT AT YEOVIL. 'AFTER EIGHT MINUTES,' RECALLED GOULD, 'HE PUT IN A THUNDERING TACKLE AND THE YEOVIL WINGER LANDED IN MY WIFE'S LAP. I SAID TO HER: "THAT'S IT. I'VE SEEN ENOUGH. WE'RE GOING HOME."'

NEWCASTLE UNITED

2008-09

- ☺ **League: 18th (Premiership)**
- ☺ **FA Cup: 0-1 Hull City, round 3 replay**
- ☺ **League Cup: 1-2 Tottenham Hotspur, round 3**

Newcastle owner Mike Ashley has always liked to be thought of as a man of the people. He wore the club strip, he sat with the fans and he guzzled beer with them. So what better gift to the people than to re-appoint Kevin Keegan as manager in January 2008 in what was hailed as the 'return of the Messiah'? Less than eight months later, however, Keegan resigned, claiming that he had not been allowed to manage. In Ashley's eyes, Keegan

KEEGAN WAS NO LONGER THE MESSIAH BUT A VERY NAUGHTY BOY

was no longer the Messiah but a very naughty boy.

The fans called for Ashley and executive director Dennis Wise to quit, prompting Ashley to stay away from home games because he thought it was unsafe to attend. Most people in his position would have sought to pacify the Toon Army with another popular managerial appointment. Instead, Ashley chose to take the opposite course of action. He appointed Joe Kinnear. He might as well have started wearing a red-and-white striped shirt.

To say the appointment of sixty-one-year-old Kinnear, who had been out of management for nearly four years, was a

It wasn't me: Joey Barton protests his innocence ... again.

surprise is like saying Roy Keane can be a bit moody. Kinnear considers himself to be a colourful character. Much the same was said about Coco the Clown. Just a week after arriving at St James' Park, Kinnear launched a foul-mouthed tirade at national journalists which made Frankie Boyle sound like the Archbishop of Canterbury. At the end of January, in a presumed attempt at levity, he mispronounced French midfielder Charles N'Zogbia's name as 'Insomnia' following defeat to Manchester City. N'Zogbia said he didn't want to play for the club again while Kinnear was in charge and was sold to Wigan the next day. Then hours before the February game with West Brom, Kinnear, who had suffered a heart attack in 1999, was rushed to hospital. His assistant Chris Hughton took over and struggling Newcastle picked up their first win since Christmas.

By the end of March, it was clear that Kinnear would not be able to return to work that season, so Ashley plucked local hero Alan Shearer from the *Match of the Day* sofa and named him interim manager. Joey Barton, who has more 'previous' than Jack the Ripper, was recalled to the side, only to be sent off in a damaging 3-0 defeat at Anfield. Afterwards, the two men exchanged words. According to press reports, Barton called Shearer 'a sh*t manager with sh*t tactics'. Outspoken as ever, Shearer told journalists that he was 'not happy'. In the event, Shearer's eight-game reign earned just five points and Newcastle were relegated after losing 1-0 at Villa Park.

⚽ ODDBALL

CHECKING IN AT THEIR SEAFRONT HOTEL BEFORE A GAME AT BRIGHTON IN NOVEMBER 1989, NEWCASTLE STAFF BEGAN UNLOADING THE TEAM KIT BASKETS FROM THE COACH ON TO A TROLLEY. BUT AS THEY WERE DOING SO, A GUST OF WIND CAUGHT HOLD OF THE TROLLEY AND SENT IT AND THE KIT BASKETS CAREERING ALONG THE PROMENADE, WHERE THEY WERE INVOLVED IN A HEAD-ON COLLISION WITH A NUMBER 67 BUS.

To round off a miserable season, it was reported that thieves had broken into St James' Park and stolen all of the club's silverware acquired over the previous thirty years – knives, forks, spoons, the lot.

NORWICH CITY

2008-09

- ⚽ **League: 22nd (Championship)**
- ⚽ **FA Cup: 0-1 Charlton Athletic, round 3 replay**
- ⚽ **League Cup: 0-1 Milton Keynes Dons, round 1**

In 2008-09 Norwich City had new shirt sponsors – insurance company Aviva. Yet given the number of times they were stuffed that season, they should really have been sponsored by Paxo. For if ever majority shareholder Delia Smith had an excuse for appearing tired and emotional on the pitch at half-time, this was it – a season that saw City demoted to the third tier for the first time in forty-nine years.

Having narrowly avoided the drop the previous season, Norwich were in trouble even before they lost 2-1 at home to ten-man Derby in October. Suspicions arose about match-fixing – because at half-time in that game, gamblers in Asia had apparently placed large sums of money on the final score. Norwich insisted there was nothing untoward; they were simply crap at defending. To underline the fact, they lost the return fixture 3-1 three weeks later.

After results failed to improve, manager Glenn Roeder left in January and was replaced on a temporary basis by the club's one-time goalkeeper, Bryan Gunn. His first match in charge saw a welcome 4-0 victory over

THE TRADITIONAL NORFOLK CELEBRATION OF HIGH SIXES

Dissatisfied customers: Norwich City season ticket holders invade the pitch to return their tickets – on the first day of the season.

Barnsley, a scoreline greeted by the traditional Norfolk celebration of high sixes. Their joy was short-lived, however, as five of City's last six games were lost – including a 3-2 setback at deadly rivals Ipswich. Escape seemed about as likely as Pot Noodle being served in the Carrow Road boardroom.

Their fate was sealed by a 4-2 final-day defeat at Charlton, who were also relegated, prompting both sets of fans to sing, 'Stand up if you're going down.' It said everything about Norwich's season that their top scorer was on-loan Reading striker Leroy Lita with seven – and he was only there for three months. Still, no doubt Aviva had the club covered against relegation.

Bizarrely, Delia and co. made Gunn's position permanent in May, only to sack him in the first week of the following season after a record 7-1 home defeat by Colchester, which saw two irate fans run on to the pitch and throw away their season tickets just twenty-two minutes into the opening day. Even for Norfolk, these were rum goings-on.

⚽ ODDBALL

IN NOVEMBER 2004, FOLLOWING A RUN OF THIRTEEN PREMIERSHIP MATCHES WITHOUT A WIN, NORWICH PLAYERS WERE URGED BY LOCAL PSYCHIC AND FAN SAMANDA CHAMBERS TO WEAR RED UNDERPANTS AS RED IS THE COLOUR OF POSITIVITY. FOR HER PART, SHE VOWED TO WEAR RED KNICKERS AT FUTURE GAMES. HER PANTIES MAY HAVE STAYED UP – BUT THE CANARIES DIDN'T.

Scotland
2008-09

Scotland's hopes of qualifying for the 2010 World Cup finals rested in the hands of manager George Burley. As it turned out, they would have been safer in the hands of Robert Green.

Three points from the opening two games against modest opponents Iceland and Macedonia made it essential that Norway were defeated at Hampden Park in October 2008. To obtain the win he desperately needed, Burley awarded Wolves' striker Chris Iwelumo his first cap at the expense of Rangers' Kris Boyd. Alas, Iwelumo marked his debut by missing a gaping goal from three yards and the match ended 0-0. After the miss, Iwelumo admitted: 'I'm my own worst critic.' Not while the Scottish media had a voice he wasn't. He went on to reveal that before the match his three-year-old daughter had told him: 'Kick the ball and score a goal.' 'If it was only that simple,' he added ruefully, leading some to question whether Burley had selected the wrong member of the family. At least Iwelumo probably had the sympathy of those in high places, as the Scottish FA chief executive at the time was Gordon Smith, whose own last-gasp miss denied Brighton

SUCCESS PROVED AS ELUSIVE AS ANDY GRAY'S FEMININE SIDE

Cup final victory against Manchester United in 1983.

Always eager to add a good scandal to abject World Cup failure, the Scots came up with Boozegate. The Rangers pair of Barry Ferguson and Allan McGregor embarked on a drinking session after the 3-0 defeat to Holland in March 2009 and were dropped by Burley for the match against Iceland four days later. They compounded their folly by making V signs from the bench to TV cameras. They were ill-equipped to play mind games.

The 2-1 victory over Iceland offered brief respite, but a 4-0 reversal in Norway and ultimately a single-goal defeat in the return fixture with the Dutch ended Scotland's chances of reaching the finals for the first time since 1998. Success had proved as elusive as Andy Gray's feminine side.

Nevertheless, the SFA backed Burley to lead the country into the Euro 2012 qualifying campaign – that is, until they suffered embarrassing friendly defeats against Japan and Wales. When your team loses 3-0 to Wales, you know your time is up. So with just three wins from his fourteen matches in charge, Burley was dismissed. During his tenure, Scotland had slipped from fourteenth in the FIFA world rankings to forty-sixth. He was not greatly mourned.

⚽ ODDBALL

RANGERS AND SCOTLAND DEFENDER KIRK BROADFOOT WAS LITERALLY LEFT WITH EGG ON HIS FACE IN 2009. HE WAS TREATED IN HOSPITAL FOR BURNS AFTER TWO POACHED EGGS HE HAD BEEN MICROWAVING EXPLODED IN HIS FACE WHEN HE OPENED THE OVEN DOOR.

Noooo: Chris Iwelumo can't believe his eyes as the ball goes almost as wide as his mouth.

LIVERPOOL

2009-10

- ⚽ **League: 7th (Premiership)**
- ⚽ **FA Cup: 1-2 Reading, round 3 replay**
- ⚽ **League Cup: 1-2 Arsenal, round 4**
- ⚽ **UEFA Champions League: 3rd in group**
- ⚽ **UEFA Europa League: 2-2 (beaten on away goal) Atlético Madrid, semi-final**

Although Liverpool hadn't won much that was worth winning for four years, manager Rafa Benitez was still in credit with the Kop, partly because of the 2005 Champions League triumph and also because he clearly wasn't overly fond of Sir Alex Ferguson. But it all began to turn sour in the summer of 2009 when playmaker Xabi Alonso was surprisingly sold to Real Madrid.

THE EUROPA LEAGUE: FOOTBALL'S EQUIVALENT OF THE REJECT BIN

At Anfield nobody was expecting the Spanish acquisition.

Benitez signed Alberto Aquilani from Roma for £17 million as Alonso's replacement, but due to injury he didn't make his League debut until November. Also sidelined for the first month of the season was Brazilian left-back Fábio Aurélio, whom Benitez had signed from Valencia in 2006. He was just returning from his latest injury when he aggravated matters playing beach football with his children. It was not the last time a beach ball would haunt Liverpool that season. Then there was Lucas Leiva, signed by Benitez in 2007.

Unlike the other two, his problem was that he was never injured. Instead, he was a player of such mediocrity that Koppites demanded to inspect his passport to make sure that he really was Brazilian.

Against this unpromising backdrop, Liverpool made a terrible start to their European campaign, losing at home to both Fiorentina and Lyon and finishing only third in their group. So they suffered the ignominy of being dumped in the Europa League, football's equivalent of the reject bin. It was like Sinatra being forced to perform in a Warrington working men's club … just before the meat raffle and bingo. Rafa's men didn't even distinguish themselves there, going out to Atlético Madrid at the semi-final stage courtesy of Manchester United old boy Diego Forlán. That went down about as well as a Steven Gerrard music request in a Southport bar.

Meanwhile, relying too heavily on Gerrard

⚽ ODDBALL

THE ONLY GOAL IN LIVERPOOL'S 1-0 DEFEAT AT SUNDERLAND ON 17 OCTOBER 2009 CAME WHEN THE BALL RICOCHETED INTO THE NET OFF A BEACH BALL. DARREN BENT'S SHOT HIT THE BRIGHT RED BEACH BALL, WHICH HAD BEEN THROWN ON TO THE PITCH BY A LIVERPOOL FAN, AND WRONG-FOOTED GOALKEEPER PEPE REINA. WHILE REINA MOVED TO HIS RIGHT TO SAVE THE BEACH BALL, THE MATCH BALL BOBBLED PAST HIM TO HIS LEFT.

and Fernando Torres, Liverpool fell at the first hurdle in the FA Cup to Championship side Reading and suffered poor League results at places like Sunderland, Fulham and Wigan. Consequently, they could finish only seventh, thereby failing to qualify for the Champions League. In June 2010, Benitez's contract was terminated.

Throughout the season, he had begun to

talk increasingly in riddles, but he surpassed himself the following October when he blamed former owners George Gillett and Tom Hicks for the club's woes and compared the team's decline to a bottle of milk. He explained: 'We have a saying in Spanish, which is, "White liquid in a bottle has to be milk."' When asked to clarify his comments, he merely added: 'White liquid in a bottle. If I see John the milkman in the Wirral, where I was living, with this bottle, I'd say: "It's milk, sure."' Thanks for clearing that up, Rafa.

Life's a beach(ball) for Liverpool's Fábio Aurélio.

SHEFFIELD WEDNESDAY

2009-10

- ☺ **League: 22nd (Championship)**
- ☺ **FA Cup: 1-2 Crystal Palace, round 3**
- ☺ **League Cup: 0-2 Port Vale, round 2**

Just as it is hard to believe that Sepp Blatter was once a lethal striker in Swiss amateur football or that Des O'Connor was a flying winger with Northampton Town, it is difficult to imagine that Sheffield Wednesday used to be a significant force in the Premier League. Between 1992 and 1994, they finished third, seventh and seventh and reached two Wembley finals, but paid the price for giving long, expensive contracts to moderate foreign imports such as Belgian striker Gilles de Bilde and Dutch forward

A WORSE INVESTMENT THAN SHARES IN NORTHERN ROCK

Gerald Sibon. These players weren't a patch on old Wednesday stalwarts like Derek Dooley – even when Dooley had only one leg!

Relegated in 2000, Wednesday were still counting the cost a decade later, by which time they were some £20 million in debt. Manager Brian Laws had acquired hero status in 2008-09 by steering Wednesday to their first League double over neighbours Sheffield United for ninety-five years, but knew all too well that such transient worship could not be trusted any more than an MP's expenses claim.

For the new season, Laws pinned much of his faith on striker Francis Jeffers, whom he

Francis Jeffers: fox in the box or toad in the road? You decide.

had signed for £700,000 in 2007. Once a precocious teenager with Everton and an £8 million signing by Arsenal, where he was known as the 'fox in the box', Jeffers had scored a total of just sixteen goals over the subsequent nine seasons for a succession of clubs, due to a combination of injury and poor form. The fox in the box was about as lively as a toad in the road. He began the 2009-10 season by being fined, banned for three matches and transfer-listed by Laws for head-butting opposing captain Tommy Fraser in a League Cup defeat to Port Vale. He went on to play a dozen League games for Wednesday that season, but predictably failed to score. His five Wednesday career goals cost £140,000 apiece (not including wages), making him a worse investment than shares in Northern Rock.

After a modest start, a mid-season run of eleven matches without a win (including four straight home defeats) meant that, sure enough, the Hillsborough fans turned on Laws and he was sacked in December following a particularly wretched 3-0 defeat at Leicester. With Wednesday in the bottom three, Laws was replaced by Alan Irvine. At first it looked as if the new broom might sweep Wednesday to safety, but there were too many cobwebs around the place and a barren spell of no wins in six left them needing to win their last game – at home to fellow strugglers Crystal Palace – to stay up. Before a crowd of 36,000, the match ended 2-2 and the Owls were relegated. The only trips the Wednesday players would be making to Wembley in the foreseeable future would be if they got tickets to see U2.

⚽ ODDBALL

WHEN BRIAN LAWS WAS MANAGER OF GRIMSBY IN 1996, HE REACTED TO DEFEAT AT LUTON BY THROWING A PLATE OF CHICKEN WINGS AT STAR STRIKER IVANO BONETTI, WHO FAILED TO DUCK OUT OF THE WAY AND SUFFERED A FRACTURED CHEEKBONE.

France
2010 WORLD CUP FINALS

Just occasionally there is poetic justice in football. So after France had qualified for the 2010 World Cup finals courtesy of Thierry Henry's handball against the Irish, few tears were shed among neutrals when they flopped in South Africa like a baguette that had been left out in the rain.

After opening their group matches with a goalless draw against Uruguay, the French camp imploded at half-time during the 2-0 defeat to Mexico. Chelsea striker Nicolas Anelka reacted angrily to criticism from coach Raymond Domenech and reportedly called him a 'son of a whore', a traditional French greeting for those occasions when a kiss on both cheeks simply won't suffice. When Anelka, who has turned sulking into an art form, refused to apologise, the French Football Federation sent him home. His teammates were so incensed by the ruling that they boycotted a training session, although their level of performance had been so woeful that it was a shock to learn they had been training at all. In their final match, they managed to lose 2-1 to hosts South Africa to finish bottom of the group.

Anelka was subsequently handed an

IT WAS A SHOCK TO LEARN THEY HAD BEEN TRAINING AT ALL

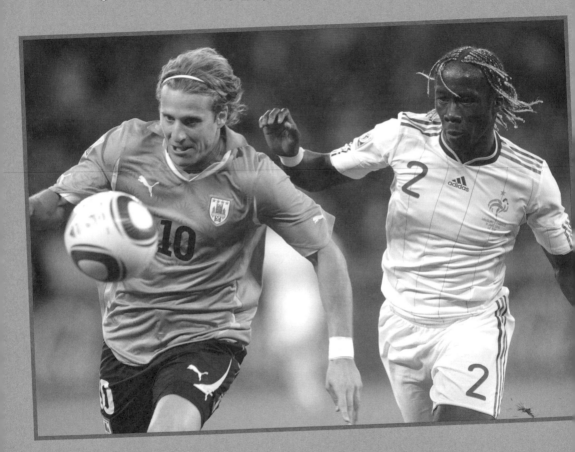

eighteen-match ban, which he said was fairly pointless because he had already decided to retire from international football. It was a classic case of who dumped whom. He called the FFF 'clowns' and claimed he was 'dying with laughter' at the decision, which everyone knew wasn't true because Anelka had never been seen to laugh.

Meanwhile the French captain, Manchester United's Patrice Evra, was banned for five games for his part in the latter-day French Revolution. As with the original, heads rolled. The President of the FFF resigned, and Domenech was replaced as coach by Laurent Blanc, who immediately suspended all twenty-three members of the World Cup squad from the next match, a friendly with Norway. Instead, Blanc wanted eleven men who were willing to lay their bodies on the line and fight for their country. It appeared a sound concept until someone pointed out to him that they had to be French.

⚽ ODDBALL

AFTER ERIC CANTONA'S INFAMOUS 1995 KUNG FU ATTACK ON A CRYSTAL PALACE FAN, A SURVEY REVEALED THAT 40 PER CENT OF BRITISH MEN WOULD RATHER GO ON HOLIDAY WITH THE FRENCHMAN THAN WITH CLAUDIA SCHIFFER.

Bonnet de douche! The French looked a right shower against Uruguay.

Italy
2010 WORLD CUP FINALS

As defending champions, Italy should have been among the favourites in South Africa, but their chances were undermined by veteran coach Marcello Lippi, who remained loyal to the core of the squad that had won the World Cup for him in 2006, despite the fact that some players were now so old, their birth certificates were written in Roman numerals. Defenders Fabio Cannavaro and Gianluca Zambrotta were thirty-six and thirty-three respectively, midfielder Mauro Camoranesi was also thirty-three, and three more members of the squad were over thirty, but

THE SINGLE-MINDEDNESS OF BERLUSCONI IN PURSUIT OF A PRETTY GIRL

Lippi resisted all calls for young blood. 'I'm not letting go of my old boys,' he vowed prior to the tournament, although an online translation service transcribed his quote as: 'I derive pleasure from holding on to my old feller.'

Lippi, who had retired as national coach following the 2006 triumph, but was persuaded back after Roberto Donadoni fared badly at Euro 2008, refused to concede that his Dad's Army was not up to the task. He demonstrated the single-mindedness of Silvio Berlusconi in pursuit of a pretty girl. Even when Italy only snatched a 1-1 draw

Ooh, me back: ageing Cannavero feels every one of his thirty-six years as he lies on the pitch.

with Paraguay thanks to a goalkeeping blunder, Lippi insisted that everything would be fine. Italy's second group opponents were New Zealand, a bunch of postmen, sheep-shearers and more sheep-shearers ranked a lowly seventy-eighth in the world. Again the Azzurri had to settle for a 1-1 draw – and even their goal was a soft penalty.

So everything boiled down to the final group match against Slovakia. Like Vanessa Feltz, the Italians have always been considered solid at the back, but on this occasion abysmal defending saw them go down 3-2. The Italians were out of the World Cup, having finished bottom of a weak group.

Lippi promptly resigned again and apologised for having selected a team 'with terror in its heart, head and legs'. The online translation service suggested that Lippi said: 'My players were scared of my legs and face.' Meanwhile the Italian media blamed the excessive number of foreign players in

⚽ ODDBALL

AS HE SCORED THE PENALTY AGAINST BRAZIL THAT EARNED ITALY A PLACE IN THE 1938 WORLD CUP FINAL, PEPPINO MEAZZA NOTICED THAT HIS SHORTS, WHICH HAD BEEN TORN EARLIER IN THE GAME, HAD SLIPPED DOWN TO HIS ANKLES. HIS CELEBRATING TEAMMATES CROWDED ROUND HIM TO SPARE HIS BLUSHES UNTIL A FRESH PAIR WERE BROUGHT ON.

Serie A. It was comforting to know that it wasn't just an English problem.

INTERNATIONALS

England
2010 WORLD CUP FINALS

Having got rid of the hapless Steve McClaren – the 'Wally with the Brolly' – following the failure to qualify for Euro 2008, it was hoped that the appointment of the no-nonsense Fabio Capello might finally bring the best out of England's overpaid Premier League stars. But after a painless qualification, when it came to South Africa the man who bears more than a passing resemblance to Sam Eagle proved himself to be just as much a muppet as his predecessor.

Before the finals, some analysts were even suggesting that England could win the tournament, although it has to be said these were the same people who still believe the Earth is flat. With no WAGs to amuse them at their Rustenburg camp, the players quickly announced that they were bored. What sort of a country was this? It was all wildlife and stuff – there wasn't even a local KFC. They carried their boredom on to the field in the opening game, drawing 1-1 with the United States after West Ham's Robert Green made the sort of fumble usually reserved for David James. A Robert Green condom was soon marketed with the slogan: 'You're guaranteed not to catch anything.'

Worse was to follow when England could

ROBERT GREEN MADE THE SORT OF FUMBLE USUALLY RESERVED FOR DAVID JAMES

only force a goalless draw with Algeria. Green was dropped for the game, but it was the outfield players who took the flak this time. Winger Aaron Lennon ran around like a headless chicken and his replacement, Shaun Wright-Phillips, played like … Shaun Wright-Phillips. As England were booed off, Wayne Rooney, who had looked particularly disinterested, had the effrontery to criticize the fans. One irate supporter found his way into the team's dressing room, thereby showing how easy it was to breach England's defence. The players responded by firmly denying that they had lost touch with the grass-roots fans – at least that's what Ashley Cole's personal shopper said in an interview with *Hello!* magazine.

Ahead of the final group match with Slovenia (whose best-known player, Robert Koren, couldn't even get in West Brom's team), there were calls for Capello to ditch the rigid 4-4-2 system and pick Joe Cole. Yes,

things were that desperate. A solitary Jermain Defoe goal saw England scrape through as group runners-up behind the USA, but this pitted them against the Germans, who ruthlessly exposed England's lumbering central defenders. Watching John Terry and Matthew Upson at top speed was like watching a pair of tortoises wading through glue.

And so England's underachievers returned home empty-handed from yet another major tournament. On landing at Heathrow, they dodged angry fans by leaving via a restricted gate. It was the best move they had put together all month.

⚽ ODDBALL

FORMER LEEDS AND ENGLAND HARD MAN DAVID BATTY WAS RESTING AT HOME WITH ANKLE LIGAMENT DAMAGE WHEN HIS TWO-YEAR-OLD DAUGHTER EXACERBATED THE INJURY BY RUNNING HIM OVER WITH HER TRICYCLE.

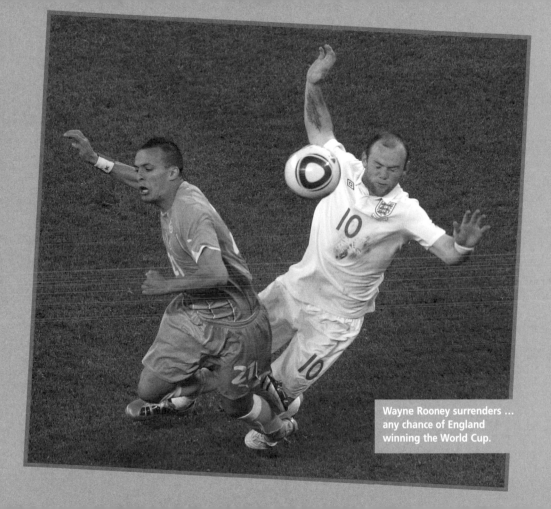

Wayne Rooney surrenders ...
any chance of England
winning the World Cup.

PRESTON NORTH END

2010-11

⚽ **League: 22nd (Championship)**
⚽ **FA Cup: 1-2 Nottingham Forest, round 3**
⚽ **League Cup: 1-2 Wigan Athletic, round 3**

Even though they last graced the top flight in 1961, the history of Preston North End has been a glorious one from the Old Invincibles of the 1880s through to wing wizard Tom Finney, the inimitable 'Preston plumber'. But 2010-11 was the season when proud Preston's form went down the drain.

Yet the season began with some optimism. Preston had been one of the better Championship sides in recent years and in Darren Ferguson (son of Sir Alex) they had a bright young manager who had enjoyed considerable success at Peterborough. And he could always call on his dad for a favour. Whereas other sons might ask for a tenner till payday or a loan towards a new car, Fergie Junior would ask his old man if he could borrow a centre-half or a striker. However, when Preston lost six of their first seven games, it became apparent that even if he had managed to borrow Rooney, Giggs, Berbatov, Van Der Sar and Vidic, the season would still have been an uphill battle.

In attack, Preston relied on the considerable presence of Jon 'The Beast' Parkin, a player who makes The Incredible Hulk look anorexic. He scored a hat-trick in

PROUD PRESTON'S FORM WENT DOWN THE DRAIN

Jon Parkin's challenge measured 7.2 on the Richter Scale.

an amazing 6-4 win at Leeds at the end of September – a match in which Preston had trailed 1-4. Alas, conceding four goals was not unusual for Preston, whose defence had enough leaks to keep Tom Finney in work for years. In midfield, meanwhile, they needed someone like West Ham's Scott Parker. Parker would definitely have improved Preston's survival chances – but then again, so would Lady Penelope.

At the end of 2010, Darren Ferguson was sacked following a home defeat to fellow strugglers Middlesbrough. Sir Alex responded by immediately recalling three of his loan players... The new manager at Deepdale was former Hull City boss Phil Brown, a manager famous for singing on the pitch and for possessing a year-round tan. The future under Brown might not have been bright, but it was certainly orange.

In fact, he had to wait until his thirteenth game in charge before eventually registering

⚽ ODDBALL

THE NINETEEN-YEAR-OLD DAVID BECKHAM SPENT A MONTH ON LOAN AT PRESTON IN MARCH 1995 AND WAS NAMED MAN-OF-THE-MATCH ON THREE OCCASIONS. A TUESDAY NIGHT GAME AT EXETER WAS WATCHED BY JUST 2,057 PEOPLE – FEWER THAN TURNED UP TO WATCH A BECKHAM LOOKALIKE OPEN A SUPERMARKET IN OXFORDSHIRE IN 2010!

a win. The 3-0 defeat of Scunthorpe on 15 March was North End's first success for over three months; a wretched run which had cast them well adrift at the foot of the table. It inspired an upturn in fortunes – but ultimately it proved too little, too late, and Preston dropped into League One.

The final ignominy came on the last day of the season, when gloating fans from local rivals Blackpool hired a plane to fly over Deepdale before the start of the game, trailing a banner that read: 'Poor Little Preston Enjoy League 1.' Brown called the stunt 'distasteful' and raged: 'If I had a gun, I'd have shot it down.' He would have needed a better aim than Preston's forwards to stand any chance of succeeding.

SOILED SHORTS

⚽ When the Namibian women's football team lost an Olympic qualifying game 13-0 to South Africa in 2003, the defeat was blamed on the girls' lust for pornography. The team's hotel bill showed that they had watched six porn films on the eve of the match before finally going to bed in the early hours of the morning.

⚽ Play was held up in the match between Scunthorpe and Rochdale in April 2004 after Rochdale keeper Neil Edwards was nipped on the arm while trying to clear a goose off the pitch.

⚽ When a match between Sheffield team Stocksbridge Steels and Witton Albion was abandoned because of thick fog in 2003, all the players trooped back to the dressing room … except for Stocksbridge goalkeeper Richard Siddall, who was unaware that the game had been called off. Unable to see beyond his penalty box, he merely assumed all the action was at the other end and stayed out on the pitch for another ten minutes before his teammates realized he was missing.

⚽ Incensed by jeering fans after a disappointing 1-1 draw with the Cape Verde Islands in a 2003 World Cup qualifier, Swaziland players suddenly ordered the driver to stop the team bus. They then jumped from the vehicle and, armed with sticks, chased their tormentors down the road.

⚽ Voted Leicester City's 1995-96 Player of the Year for his safe hands, goalkeeper Kevin Poole was presented with a cut-glass rose bowl … which he promptly dropped.

⚽ After Algeria had been knocked out of the qualifying rounds for the 1998 World Cup, the country's king was so angry that he banned the coach and his deputy from football for life and disbanded the National League.

⚽ On 2 April 1994 Scottish club Cowdenbeath beat Arbroath 1-0 to end a two-year run of thirty-eight home League games without a win.

⚽ While filming an advert in 2004, Brazilian soccer star Ronaldinho fluffed an overhead kick and ended up smashing a window at a twelfth-century Madrid cathedral.

⚽ Having lost all fourteen games at the start of the 1993-94 season, Thetford Town players were hypnotized in an attempt to improve their fortunes. They lost their next game 9-0.

⚽ After scoring from the penalty spot in 2004, Bayer Leverkusen goalkeeper Joerg Butt took so long to return to his goal following his celebrations that Schalke striker Mike Hanker scored from the centre circle direct from the restart.

⚽ During a game between Belgian teams Young Stars Eeklo and FC Zelzate in 2004 a fan ran on to the pitch and pulled down the shorts and pants of referee Jacky Temmerman.

⚽ A Somerset footballer hit a crucial penalty over the bar after a female opposition supporter flashed her breasts at him from behind the goal. With the game finishing 0-0 after extra time, the 2003 Morland Challenge Cup Final between Norton Hill Rangers and Wookey FC went to penalties. Cruelly distracted by a woman lifting her shirt as he ran up to the ball, a Rangers player ballooned his spot kick into the car park, allowing Wookey to triumph 3-2. A spot of 'Wookey nookie' had won the day …

⚽ Norwegian referee Per Arne Brataas confessed in 2003 that he tried to avoid handing out red and yellow cards because he suffers from dyslexia and can't face writing post-match reports.

⚽ The Wheatsheaf pub team from St Helen's Auckland, County Durham, achieved the distinction of finishing the 1994-95 season with fewer points than they started with. They drew one and lost the other twenty-nine League games, but were also docked two points for failing to field a team on one occasion. So they ended up with a points total of minus one.

⚽ Montserrat were officially named the worst national team in the world in 2002. In the play-off for last place Montserrat, 203rd in the FIFA rankings, were beaten 4-0 by the Himalayan kingdom of Bhutan, ranked one position higher. A crowd of 25,000 masochists turned up to witness the clash of the clueless.

⚽ Midfielder Paulo Diogo of Swiss club Servette scored against Schaffhausen in 2004 and promptly jumped into the crowd to celebrate. In doing so, he caught his wedding ring on a fence and tore off the top half of his finger. He was then booked by the referee for excessive celebration.

⚽ Holidaymaker Andrew Amers-Morrison was appointed manager of the Seychelles' national team in 2010 after the country's football association mistook him for former Manchester City defender Andy Morrison. Even on discovering their blunder, the SFA gave him six months to prove he could do the job.

⚽ A Brazilian referee was left with a red face after pulling a pair of red lacy knickers from his pocket instead of a red card during a match in 2004. Carlos Jose Figueira Ferro was trying to send off a player during an amateur match in Anama, but was so embarrassed by his gaffe that he ended the match twenty minutes early. His wife, who was watching, did see red, however, and was reported to be starting divorce proceedings.

PICTURE ACKNOWLEDGEMENTS

Page 13	Mark Leech/Offside
Page 16	Mark Leech/Offside
Page 19	Mark Leech/Offside
Page 22	Russell Cheyne/Allsport/Getty Images
Page 25	Neal Simpson/EMPICS/PA Images
Page 28	Mark Leech/Offside
Page 31	PA Archive/PA Images
Page 34	EMPICS/PA Images
Page 37	Bob Thomas/Getty Images
Page 40	Phil O'Brien/EMPICS/PA Images
Page 43	Ross Kinnaird/EMPICS/PA Images
Page 46	Matthew Ashton/EMPICS/PA Images
Page 48	Ross Kinnaird/EMPICS/PA Images
Pages 52-3	Ross Kinnaird/EMPICS/PA Images
Page 55	Steve Morton/EMPICS/PA Images
Page 59	Laurence Griffiths/EMPICS/PA Images
Page 61	Steve Morton/EMPICS/PA Images
Pages 64-5	David Kendall/PA Archive/PA Images
Page 67	Neal Simpson/EMPICS/PA Images
Page 69	David Kendall/PA Archive/PA Images
Page 72	Barry Coombs/EMPICS/PA Images
Page 75	David Cheskin/PA Archive/PA Images
Page 78	Tony Marshall/EMPICS/PA Images
Page 82	Ben Radford/Allsport/Getty Images
Page 85	Matthew Ashton/EMPICS/PA Images
Page 88	ABACA/PA Images
Page 91	Matthew Ashton/EMPICS/PA Images
Page 93	Mike Egerton/EMPICS/PA Images
Page 96	David Davies/PA Archive/PA Images
Page 99	Tony Marshall/EMPICS/PA Images
Page 103	John Walton/EMPICS/PA Images
Page 106	Michael Cooper/EMPICS/PA Images
Page 109	Mike Hewitt/Getty Images
Page 111	Jill Jennings/Haymarket/PA Images
Page 113	John Walton/EMPICS/PA Images
Pages 116-7	Mike Egerton/EMPICS/PA Images
Page 120	Barry Coombs/EMPICS/PA Images
Page 123	Nick Potts/PA Archive/PA Images
Page 125	Stephen Pond/EMPICS/PA Images
Page 128	Peter Byrne/PA Archive/PA Images
Page 131	Chris Radburn/PA Archive/PA Images
Page 135	Andrew Milligan/PA Archive/PA Images
Pages 138-9	Simon Bellis/Landov/PA Images
Page 141	John Walton/EMPICS/PA Images
Page 144	Henri Szwarc/ABACA/PA Images
Page 147	Bernat Armangue/AP/PA Images
Page 151	Roberto Candia/AP/PA Images
Page 153	PA Wire/PA Archive/PA Images